THE FOUR PER CENT

Locked down but left out during
Melbourne's Covid response

LAUREN SMITH

Copyright © Lauren Smith, 2024

The moral rights of the author have been asserted. All rights reserved. No part of this publication may be reproduced, distributed, or transmitted in any form or by any means, including photocopying, recording, or other electronic or mechanical means, without the prior written permission of the publisher, except as permitted under the *Copyright Act 1968*.

ISBN: (Print) 978-0-6459237-3-5
            (eBook) 978-0-6459237-4-2

 A catalogue record for this book is available from the National Library of Australia

Editing: Kellie Nissen (https://justrightwords.com.au/)

Cover and inside pages design: Claire McGregor (https://clairemcgregor.com.au)

Author photograph: Myphotocosy

Author's note

The Four Per Cent was written and edited between September 2022 and April 2024. Even within that period, 'statistics' changed and new information emerged, and continues to do so. There was a point where I had to stop amending and send the manuscript to the printer. It should also be noted that different sources may interpret 'known information' differently. As you read this book, be mindful of the changing nature of 'facts' and use the information here as a guide only. You can access up-to-date information via the websites listed in the endnotes.

This book is one person's perspective on life and how best to live it and does not aim to substitute for professional medical advice, diagnosis or treatment. Always seek the advice of your qualified health care provider with any questions you may have regarding a medical condition or treatment and before undertaking a new health care regimen.

Each individual has their own unique makeup and understanding of their health and wellness. Each individual is on their own physical and mental health journey and only they can best establish a team of people and a toolkit of resources that service their own needs.

If any information contained within this book brings up issues for you, please contact LIFELINE in Australia on 13 11 14. If you are outside Australia, please contact your local recommended mental health resources. Do not suffer alone.

Contents

Author's note	iii
Preface	1
About me	5
The importance of writing	8
Your turn	*13*
A commitment to yourself	15
Why write about Covid?	17
Your turn	*19*
Think about what you wrote	*21*
Why put this into a book?	22
The importance of shifting pain from our bodies	25
Using this book	27
Part 1: The Covid pandemic lockdown in Melbourne	**29**
The significant dates	*30*
Questions to ponder	*34*
Lockdown	*34*
Reopening	*40*
A quick summary	*44*
Ongoing restrictions	*44*
Part 2: My story	**47**
Living with Trigeminal neuralgia	*47*
Your turn	*63*
When Covid hit	*65*
Mandates	*67*
Unpopular decision	*69*
Reopening	*71*
2022 letter from neurologist	*75*
Still no exemption	*78*
Facing the reality	*78*
Hospitalisation	*79*
Thailand	*82*

After everything … 88
Your turn 89
My Melbourne – then and now 91
Your turn 95

Part 3: The lessons 97
Your turn 101
How did we get here? 103
Your turn 106
How we speak matters 108

Lesson 1: Validation 110
Your turn 116

Lesson 2: Connection 118
Your turn 124

Lesson 3: Fear 126
Your turn 129

Lesson 4: Reality versus truth – our need to be right 131
Your turn 135

Lesson 5: Having an opinion 137
Your turn 141

Lesson 6: The mass contradiction 143
Your turn 146

Lesson 7: Guilt as motivation 148
Your turn 152

Lesson 8: Better leadership 154
Your turn 158

Lesson 9: Where did the stress on the hospital system come from? 160
Your turn 166

Lesson 10: Staying well 168
Your turn 171

Lesson 11: Less entitlement, more love 173
Your turn 175

Lesson 12: What to trust	177
Your turn	*180*
Lesson 13: Everyone has a different experience of this time	182
Your turn	*185*
Part 4: Where to from here?	187
Your turn	*195*
What else might you start questioning?	*197*
How to move forward	202
Your turn	*206*
And my point is …	208
Your turn	*213*
Final words	215
Acknowledgments	217
Where to go for more information	221
Endnotes	*223*
About the author	228

Preface

Here I am, writing a book.

I can't say it was ever on my radar and I honestly can't believe I'm actually doing it. I've never considered myself an author. My sloppy grammar and misplaced punctuation proves that – but does that matter? How I write is truly me and it is how I choose to speak my truth into existence.

If I look back on my life – both personal and professional – the fact I've chosen to put pen to paper in this way shouldn't surprise me. Storytelling in some form has always been my mode of expression. It's both my greatest strength and biggest enemy. It's been the constant in my darkest times and the revealer of my honest feelings at those times I struggle to express them in person.

When I first sat down to start writing this, sitting in my inner-eastern rental in Melbourne, Australia, it was 2022 – my fortieth year on this planet. I was still suffering the effects of the global pandemic. I'd recently sold my apartment and closed my business, having barely survived six lockdowns, totalling over three hundred and forty days, without being able to offer in-person services.

Rarely able to leave the house in that two-year period, I'd had a lot of time to think about my life. As I grappled with the recent changes, I also realised I'd packed quite a lot into my forty years. I've seen a few things. I've definitely made mistakes. I've learned a thing or two about the world and, more importantly, about myself and my place on this earth.

Right now, I'm choosing to take the opportunity to tell my story. To talk about some of the things I've most recently observed. If I had to pick from the topics heavily pushed in the five years prior to the Covid pandemic, they would centre around the following: saving the planet; providing spaces of support and inclusion; mental health; eliminating stigmas; and encouraging people to speak about their traumas and command autonomy over their bodies. It would be a call to be an ally on many fronts and show you care about these issues by actively calling out your own friends, family and work colleagues and beginning conversations that educate others in the above spaces.

In this time, there has also been a wave of momentum, with the general population coming to an accepting space where they understand everyone has a different life, a different way they see the world and a different ability to experience it. Up until 2020, it felt like we were moving in the right direction.

Were we still getting things wrong? Absolutely.

Was there still much that needed to be discussed in these areas? Of course there was.

Conversation on both sides has always been key to change. But an ability to speak up and talk through our fears was becoming the new accepted norm. We were taking steps towards understanding one another and appreciating we could all exist while not being the same. As the Ted talks told us, we were moving towards 'ideas worth spreading'. Moving towards creating space for individuals to be both challenged in their thinking while continuing to hold space for their views. We were on our way to seeing that mutual understanding – or just simple respect – could exist between two people who sat on opposite sides of a fence but both equally cared to water and look after the grass as their own. In addition, there was also a massive push in education with less space for judgement.

There was a growing ability to listen to understand. A new generation of people who were either healing the traumas of their past generations or raising children who knew it was okay to seek support and deal with their issues, without it being seen as a sign of weakness.

We can all relate to a moment that felt like this in those prior years. Maybe you were one of very few females in your office and benefited from the strength of other woman finally coming forward to say the way they were treated wasn't acceptable. Maybe you suffered your own mental challenges in silence and suddenly felt comfortable to talk about them in general conversation, knowing you weren't alone. Maybe you were grateful that your child was recognised for their unique talents instead of being pushed towards academic prowess in areas that didn't interest them.

As we moved forward, some of these new ways of thinking were a blessing in disguise after the internal struggles we'd faced our whole lives. Some challenged our beliefs and made us face who we thought we were. Some made us acknowledge that it had gone too far. At the very least, it sparked discussion. Different thoughts, opinions and ways of living were finally being talked about and someone, somewhere, in each situation felt like they were finally being heard, rather than demonised for not agreeing with the majority or having to suffer in silence.

Then Covid hit.

In an instant, it was like none of these things mattered anymore. In fact, we went backwards.

Suddenly, people needed to suck it up.

People needed to do what they were told without question.

Some people were ostracised for their choices. Labelled as extremists. Made to feel guilty if they weren't coping while others in 'harder situations' were.

We went from living in a society that prided itself on understanding, empathy, learning from past mistakes and rejecting previous black-and-white thinking, to a society with a hard line drawn down the centre and no margin for middle ground. There were only two options: doing your bit to protect everyone else or trying to kill grandma. Any suggestion to have a conversation or discussion was labelled conspiracy.

Some will look back on this time and still decide they were the heroes because they did everything they were asked to save a generation of grandparents who ultimately died in the end of loneliness and a broken heart. However, as the years go on, many people will erase this point of time from their minds and not learn the lessons from it. Why? Because the honest representation of who they became during this period will be too painful to remember. They will sit on the wrong side of history. Many will have easily forgotten their strongly held views, while complaining about countries that still hadn't fully opened up, robbing them of their blissfully ignorant holiday being served by those whose vax status they didn't even know. Closer to home, you may find them asking why people are still wearing masks at the supermarket, muttering "Don't they know it's over?" and conveniently forgetting that just because the media isn't reporting daily case numbers doesn't mean that it's gone away.

In fact, it's worse.

It's interesting the stories people tell themselves when they decide which parts of it are preventing them from living their life the way they want.

Just as dangerous as the people who mysteriously forgot the words they were spruiking a few months earlier are the people who felt the need to silence their voice entirely.

That honest representation of who we let ourselves become falls hardest on the ones that did what was right but allowed themselves to be shamed for it. The ones that listened to the haters and lost themselves in the process. Who became too fragile to speak for fear of prosecution. The ones who questioned themselves for so long they forgot who they were. The ones who knew they had a lot to say, had good reason for it and understood the importance of sharing a lived experience among the fearmongers screaming the loudest. But yet, they didn't. They allowed themselves to be embarrassed by their stories. They doubted their own truths. They felt they had no power over their own lives. When they opened their mouths, they couldn't find the words.

Until today.

About me

I was born in Morwell in Gippsland, country Victoria, the youngest of three daughters. Arriving eight-and-a-half years after my middle sister, the generation gap meant I was the only one who bucked the white picket fence tradition by going to uni and moving to 'the big smoke' of Melbourne.

My seventy-six-year-old father is a retired power station plant operator of forty-three years. He only completed Grade 6 as education was deemed irrelevant for a family of fourteen who were surviving in a three-bedroom commission house. My seventy-two-year-old mother left school in Year 9, becoming a checkout chick before dedicating her life to being a stay-at-home mum and, later, a carer for those most important to her.

My parents still live in the same house I was likely conceived in. I don't believe I will ever know another place that they call home. They are the most reliable people I know, with very solid foundations of who they are. Their house is a home – an obvious love of one place, surrounded by the things they know make sense to them. My father has woken to eat his All-Bran cereal and read the *Herald Sun*, cover to cover, every single day of his life. My mother has dinner on the table at 6 pm every night, without fail. If, by some colossal tragedy, she isn't home, the pots and pans, and all the cut vegies bobbing in the water, are ready to go.

From these very solid parents, I somehow rejected normalcy and structure. Or, I simply had no interest in keeping up with the country town Jones. After moving to Melbourne at the age of twenty, I worked first as a television editor and producer, freelancing for most of the major networks in Australia and sometimes overseas. I went on to become a Pilates and yoga instructor, opened a studio and ran wellness retreats, both here and abroad. I've also run a business as a manual driving instructor, and volunteered on the committee of an organisation who rehome displaced young people. Currently, I call Thailand home. And, in amongst all of this, I'm somehow moonlighting as the author of this book.

I am single. I never married. I don't have children. I don't feel defined by the job I have, my financial status, any material possessions or where I live. I'm simply a human being experiencing life just as each of us is, and I'm trying to do it in a way that feels right for me.

I've studied many things and have a deep desire to know how the world truly works and my place in it. From my varied careers, two businesses and multiple trips overseas, I've been exposed to all spectrums of people, cultures, generations and life experiences. I've been 'friends' with those who wouldn't give you $5 of their million, and others who would literally give you the shirt off their back without being in a position to replace it.

I've decided that, in this world, there are three groups of people. The first two are the ones who think life happens to them, and the ones who make it happen, concentrating on what they can, despite their situation. The third group has the awareness of both but allows the thoughts in their head decide the kind of day they are having. They know the answer lives within them, yet, equally feel they have no power to do anything about it.

My life has been a journey of both extremes. In the last three years, however, I've sat solidly in the third group – a place where I think a lot of prior self-motivators sit. Those people who, post-Covid, are now struggling to find a way to continue the way they used to because they've been beaten down by the system. It's a place that does none of us any favours.

Is any of that really important?

Is it relevant in this book?

Maybe in another time it has been – but not now. Right now, there is only one thing you really need to know about me.

I am one of the four per cent.

What does that mean? Four per cent of what?

Quite simply, I am one of the four per cent of eligible people in Melbourne who chose not to be vaccinated during the Covid pandemic.[1]

As my story begins, I want to make it clear that I *chose* not to get vaccinated.

I am one of the four per cent who was used as a reason to keep Melbourne – where I lived – locked down longer.

One of the four per cent who was labelled everything – selfish, deranged, a conspiracy theorist, a threat to public safety and someone who deserved whatever was coming to them, even death.

A person who had to listen to every individual's strongly held opinion on how dangerous a person like me is to society. These opinions didn't only come from faceless keyboard warriors, but from those I'd known all my life.

A person who, in late 2023, was still not allowed to work in some everyday businesses, not allowed to walk into some high-risk areas and who will not be considered for organ transplant if, God forbid, that is needed at any time soon.

All of this despite never once having had Covid.

This is my story of how that decision, which was and remains the right decision for me, deeply affected my life and continues to do so in so many ways.

The importance of writing

Writing, in some form, has always been a crucial part of my life and the way I choose to express myself.

As a child, my desire to share stories began when I created my version of the 'choose your own adventure' books, along with board games with TV trivia questions and activities.

As a young student, I was a note-taker and would often make up riddles or rhymes using each first letter of a piece of information that was imperative to remember.

In my high school years, I entered singing competitions but was never happy with choosing just one song. I'd find the constant thread in a variety of music and piece them together to tell one story via my voice.

In my early working life, I was the editor of my university's student magazine. From there, I was paid to monitor mentions in the media for both private companies and governments, advising whether the general public's opinion of them was positive or negative. I went on to make a living as a television editor, EVS operator and, later, a producer. For fifteen years I told daily stories through this visual medium; firstly in news, then sports. I aimed to find the human interest, wanting most to speak for those who couldn't or didn't know how. In my wellness business, I listened to other people's stories every day. I gave them the tools to help shape their lives through movement, mindset and mindfulness. I guided them to be the creator of their own stories, through these mediums.

Even as a driving instructor, I used the stories my clients told me of their fears on the road to help navigate a safe rite of passage for each individual, in a way they best understood. I often asked them: "What can you do in this situation?"

To put the power back into the hands of others builds confidence; it elicits thought, growth and resilience. Each day, we can learn something different about ourselves in the stories of our own lives.

The therapeutic benefits of writing, of expressing my thoughts and feelings while questioning the doubts in my head, were well understood by my mind and body long before I discovered the science that shows just how important it is. For me, this honest expression has cemented some of my favourite memories and changed the course of the most important relationships in my life.

My first attempt at baring my soul through the words on a page was in my early twenties where I used the images from existing *Mr. Men* and *Little Miss* children's books but changed the words to tell my own story. I wrote them as gifts for two different friends, in two different genres, and for two very different reasons. One was a funny tale for a friend's birthday, with all the characters comprising members of our workplace and their annoying traits. The other was equal parts heartache and admiration for a dear friend who was about to take the biggest step in their life to advance their career. Sadly, this meant I wouldn't see them anymore. I used the words of that book to explain how much my heart was breaking over that thought; to convey how much they actually meant to me, as I could never find the words to say it to their face.

I often think about that last book when I see a piece of *Mr. Men* memorabilia. It makes me remember that doing this, writing those little books for friends, was what started the trajectory of getting my deepest thoughts out on paper. Saying exactly what I felt deep inside was a vital experience for my own mental health. It released the stored tension in my body and helped me process what I was feeling. It was freeing to be me, to be honest, to be raw. That one little cut-and-paste children's book changed that relationship forever. It was the right decision to speak up and tell them what I felt and, to this day, that one act of bravery almost twenty years ago still makes me smile. With a marketing influx and a fifty-year reunion of *Mr. Men* and *Little Miss* exploding in front of me, it's been a timely reminder that I have to be brave again – now.

I write this knowing not all pivotal moments in my life, where honest feelings were expressed, resulted in a positive result. However, I wouldn't have done them differently. As difficult as those moments were, they either propelled me forward in a direction I needed to go or dragged me away from what should stay in the past. There are moments where I feel bad for what was said. Moments where I know, in hindsight, I could have chosen different language to express how I felt without passing judgement or letting my ego take over. Back then, I didn't have the knowledge or perspective to do better, but the growth I've gained since tells me all situations needed to happen the way they did. Any lost relationships that are still worth having either did, or will eventually, find their way back at the right time.

Those honest letters have been responsible for making my mother inconsolable, ending my relationship with my best friend of eighteen years, and expressing how lonely or forgotten I felt within close friendships or loving relationships.

Early on, those honest letters were written from a victim's perspective. I wanted those around me to change for the betterment of my own life. None of those people were responsible for my feelings; it was the person I battled inside my head who was responsible. Each written word helped me see that.

The more I grew comfortable with who I was, the more I understood that only I am responsible for how thoughts are shaped inside my head. It's up to me to deal with my past traumas, to challenge my strongly held black-and-white views, to understand how my own journey has shaped the way I see things, and that I can only change that perspective once I've had the chance to speak about my fears, to listen and process opposing information and to stay curious in my quest to learn and do better. Through this cathartic growth process came the understanding that everyone is just doing the best they can in any situation with the knowledge and resources currently at their disposal. This includes me.

Later letters I wrote became a more fact-based expression of my feelings – but now with less judgement and no expectation of the result. Honest letters that expressed my boundaries regarding what I was willing to put up with as a person, and communicating what most needed to be said. Some letters were a little more inflammatory than others but most had the desired result – they stopped people in their tracks, called them out on their behaviour or expressed the regret I had for my own failings.

These letters elicited genuine apologies, prompted deep conversations, and provided an ability to work out any miscommunication or understanding. They sought closure through final statements and, at times, prompted no response at all. Sometimes, that's all that was needed.

With each piece I've written, my hope was they would eventually help others as much as they helped me. Every piece of writing helped me process strong emotions, helped me get those feelings out of my head and into words that I could decipher and make sense of, helped move stuck energy out of my body along with feelings of anger, helplessness and loss.

My writing helped me communicate how I was feeling and how I wanted to feel. I was able to deal with situations that, at first, seemed beyond my realm of understanding or ability to move past.

In my attempt to do this for myself once again, this book will ask you to do the same.

For me it's a healing exercise.

What it is for you is your choice.

Just like a journal, the idea is to provide space for you to write what you feel about each chapter and the subject discussed. Has it lit a fire within you? What do you feel it's saying? What emotions has it stirred up? Do you feel validated within each sentence? Are you completely over the topic I'm about to address, perhaps because you haven't truly dealt with it and therefore can't bear to read another word?

This is your chance to ask yourself 'why?' and to consider all the questions you've had. Then perhaps for once we can all fully move on from the recent challenges of our lives.

This book is multi-faceted. On the surface, it's my truth. The truth of what happened during Melbourne's Covid times. Ultimately, though, it's a cry for freedom. The freedom for people to feel. To write. To ask questions about the things they don't understand instead of feeling the need to pick a side.

With the current state of the world, we really need that freedom right now.

Your turn

What do you hope to get out of this book? What are your expectations? Right now, what do you most need to honour about your own story?

The Four Per Cent

A commitment to yourself

*To effect any change, we need to first make
a commitment to and for ourselves.
This is the commitment I hope you make for yourself.*

I hope you take this chance to write down what you feel.

We all need to truly acknowledge, accept, forgive and move on from this part of our history. A lot of people have already blocked those years out, trying to convince themselves it wasn't as bad as it was, that everything is now fine and we can all just pick up and move on.

While I don't want to be stuck in a moment of time that I'll blame for all my failings for years to come, truly moving on from something only happens when we acknowledge the hurt and pain it has caused for us as well as others. Moving on happens when we realise what we can learn from the experience, so we don't make similar mistakes in the future. Moving on happens when we validate the feelings associated with the time and process the changes it has made to our lives.

When it comes to change, the Covid experience made quite a lot.

The current tension we are all feeling is a bundle of unprocessed trauma over many things. People are angrier. They are tired. There are less pleasantries. The world is stressed in many ways and we need to talk about how this heaviness affects us if we don't try to move it. So, why not start with something we all went through?

Any person, anywhere in the world, could pick this book up and tell their story of this point in time. It's not limited to a particular experience to which only some people can relate. It is something all of us have gone through.

Worldwide, each person alive between late 2019 and early 2023 has their own genuine experience of the same global event. This fact in itself demonstrates the enormity of this event. Don't talk yourself out of that. Don't play it down. We all went through some heavy shit, maybe at different times and in different ways over those three-plus years, but we all have an individual experience of a time in history that affected each and every person alive on earth. That is a big deal, it has stirred some big feelings and they need to be addressed.

I need to address the hurt, the feelings and the strong emotions I went through from my perspective. Somewhere in my words you may relate, or you may disagree. More importantly, you'll add your own – that's what the space is for.

This book is me processing the last three-plus years and also an invitation for you to do the same in your own words. Don't feel like each line is a chance for a rebuttal. Focus less on trying to discredit my thoughts and more on just speaking your truth, whatever it is. It might be very different, it may have similarities but in the end, it's your story to tell.

So, I want a commitment from you to do the work on the following pages. This commitment really is to yourself. Honour it. If you are not ready, come back when you are. I'll still be here when you are ready to show up for yourself.

Why write about Covid?

Indeed – why? The whole pandemic was a long time ago, wasn't it? The lockdowns? The daily numbers? All in the past.

Well, no.

And that's not really what this book is about anyway. We all have our own experiences. Our own opinions and ideas and memories of that time. The past years, the world and the media may have moved on but for some – many – of us, it's far from over. And the conversations have barely begun.

What I will be discussing is less about whether it was right to do what was done and more about the feelings associated with why you individually chose the decision you felt was right for you at the time.

That's right – we can't deny we all had a part in this, and while I know some may not agree with me, every individual will have their own truth of the experience. Our truth will fluctuate from the actual reality of the situation because of the feelings that we chose to focus on in that exact moment. There will be the reality – the absolute fact – of the situation. And there will be your truth or your reason – based on your most dominant feeling – for why you responded, reacted and processed the events in the way you did.

Some of you will say you acted in certain ways 'because I was forced'. I appreciate and do not deny that. Within that reality, however, in making the decisions you did, there would have been a feeling: fear about losing money; guilt of spreading Covid to others; hopelessness of thinking you can't win either way.

The reality of the situation and each person's truth around it are different things, so please do not confuse them. This book is an opportunity to listen to another's perspective. And, it is an opportunity to share and acknowledge your own.

Here's my perspective:

I chose not to get vaccinated against Covid because it was going to do me more harm than good.

Your turn

At this very point in time, you do not yet know my reason for the choice I made. How does it make you feel, though? Right now, I want you to write down your instant reaction to reading these words: not vaccinated.

The Four Per Cent

Think about what you wrote

Did you get it all out?

Did you explain every uncomfortable knot in your stomach and any rash judgement that sprung into your head? Maybe you were completely relieved to find someone else the same as you. Maybe you were furious and felt the need to throw this book down.

If enough time has passed for you and you no longer care but once did, I invite you to continue writing but, this time, focus on what you would have said if you'd heard me say the same thing twelve or eighteen months ago. Or longer.

Be honest.

For some, you'll need only go back on your social media posts to see the strongly held opinions you expressed at that time. Believe me, I saw them. All of them. So many of those publicly-expressed opinions remain in the screen shots of my phone as a reminder that I wasn't going crazy back then. That I truly was, and am still, being gaslit by those who have since chosen to ignore the part they played in dehumanising an entire section of the community. I'm not saying 'you were wrong', but sharing this as a means of providing a learning experience; one where you can show your own growth or changed opinion on this topic. I also want to point out how dangerous it can be to simply react, rather than observe and process. And to demonstrate how little you can understand about a person's reason for their own choices in life, yet how easy it is to jump on the train of outrage without ever asking them why.

Why put this into a book?

There are many reasons for writing a book. Ultimately, though, it boils down to two intentions – to process your own thoughts, ideas and experiences; and to be thought-provoking and open up a pathway for conversation.

When I started writing this book, it was to get all the thoughts out of my head – the ones that already existed and the ones that grew during the Covid years, and beyond. With the world becoming more divided, I've found a greater need to process parts of my life that still upset me. Each topic left unprocessed snowballs into the next and, with the state of the world, I don't need that in my life. I was writing from the deep-down, dark place that exists inside of me and needed answers. The place I'd been bogged down in and now needed to move through.

If nothing else, this whole situation reminded me that it was time to be done with the 'no control' part of my life. It was time to move on to bigger and better things. There were a few jobs I thought I would excel at but, sadly, vaccination status was still asked for and it was obvious that despite the world looking like it was over the mandates, it's still just a hidden uncomfortable conversation that people assume they won't have to have that often. No-one has put their foot down and said, "Enough is enough".

The bias very much still exists.

So I started to write about it and I kept writing about it. In doing so, I felt the pressure of needing to do something for the good of others but, at the same time, there was also a dangerous amount of regret for not standing up for myself at the time. For doing everything quietly. For not wanting to rock the boat. For years of pretending I was someone I wasn't. For the situation I eventually found myself in –

injured, both physically due to job and lifestyle changes arising from mandate restrictions, and mentally, for allowing the loudest voices to crush my soul.

Many times, I have stopped typing. I've closed the computer screen, paced around the house, made trips to the kitchen for drinks and snacks because my brain simply does not want to talk about pain and food is my coping mechanism.

Many times, I've cried myself to sleep for letting myself sink as low as I had. Many times, I decided that I can't do this, I'm still not mentally prepared. I'm not ready to relive the trauma.

I wrote this knowing that it might be a long road dealing with the fallout from it but I wrote it all the same. I wrote to try and find the confident person who went missing. The one who trusts in herself more than anything else. I've survived my worst days and I'm still here. I am solely in control of my own life and there is power in that. I just need to find it in myself.

As I wrote, I realised I was also writing this book for you. To be the kick in the guts you need. The calling out of bullshit you need. The self-audit. The spiritual, but not religious, look at your connection to self and others. A self-help guide. The nudge that changes you from a fixed mindset to a growth mindset. Something to make you change your thoughts from negative to positive. From being in lack to being in abundance. This book is asking you to start today. To forgive yourself for not doing it sooner but to start where you are. To show you that love is the only answer – unconditional love for yourself and love for others. Forget the gossiping. Don't do the "Oh my God, did you see what … blah blah?" Do the "Oh my God, what can we do about this in a constructive way?"

Am I writing this book for myself, to shift the feelings that, on some days, make me wonder if it's even worth it anymore? Yes.

Am I also writing it for all of you, for the same reasons? Yes.

The most important thing to know about this book is there is no right or wrong answer. I have my story to tell and you have yours. We all need to process the hurt now because none of us have. We need to learn now how important it is to deal with feelings as they come up. It may seem harder. It may take longer. It's not a natural response. When it becomes a natural response it will be easier.

But you have to change that first.

The importance of shifting pain from our bodies

When we don't ignore what we went through – when we have the hard conversations that need to be had, sometimes if only with ourselves – we don't need to be tough and suck it up. We need to talk about it. We need to open our minds to different opinions and understand that we all went through a hard time.

Everyone lost something in this process, just not the same thing. We need to stop holding on to the 'us versus them' mentality and its various examples, not only throughout this pandemic but life in general. The more you try to push it down as if it didn't exist, the more it buries deep in the recesses of your soul, waiting to find an imperfect opportunity to subconsciously rush out.

We tend to allow our minds to simply ignore the mistakes we make because we can't find a way to apologise for them. That would involve having to address who we really are and whether it marries with who we tell ourselves we want to be.

We act as if the idea of saying 'I'm sorry' is the worst thing a human being could possibly go through.

Let me tell you it's actually the opposite.

Saying sorry is one of the more cathartic experiences. Take all your ailments, illnesses and stress that constantly lives in your body, that negative energy you can't find a reason for, and realise it's the physical presentation of your bullshit asking to be called out. How much more darkness and uncomfortable energy do you want to carry around with you in these times? How many more excuses can you make for not taking ownership of your life? How much longer are you willing to put up with the impact you have on yourself and those around you?

Throughout history, we look back at times where we've made massive mistakes, caused losses of lives, and dehumanised people – and sixty years later, we're waiting for the next generation to apologise on our behalf. I bet it didn't take you sixty years to realise it was wrong, but it took you sixty years to admit you were a part of it, or worse, say it had nothing to do with you. We are not complicit because we were 'just doing what we were told'. How many people could you have positively affected during those sixty years if you just said sorry or had a hard conversation to address the elephant in the room? How much more of a positive experience could you have had in your own life if you just learned the lesson, processed it and moved on, without carrying the weight of guilt or regret around with you? Have you lived your life trying to make up for your failings without first forgiving yourself?

Think of the pressure on your broken-down physical body. Think of those unaddressed thoughts that keep you awake at night. Think of the elephant expression literally! Why would anyone let an elephant stay in a room? Wouldn't you be doing anything you could to get it out? How much heaviness have you allowed yourself to be weighed down by without the acknowledgement that no-one is going to move it but you?

So take some weight off. I certainly am.

Using this book

The words contained on the following pages are a true and accurate account of my life in the years during, and after, the Covid pandemic.

The feelings that come up for you as you read these words will be yours to process accordingly. This book, and the journaling pages I've included, will give you the space to do just that.

At no point are you invited to decide that my feelings are wrong, for it's not your story. You may not like what I say. My ideas and experiences may make you uncomfortable, and that is fine, but I want you to ask yourself why?

On the other hand, you may relate and it may become an opportunity for you to finally get everything off your own chest. A moment to tell your story, one that is uniquely yours. No-one can take that away from you.

It may be an opportunity to grow, to release, to further dig in the heels of your black-and-white thinking.

However you experience this book, I want you to do one thing – use the journal pages to express how you feel in that moment. Then use those words to work out where to go with that knowledge. Can you learn from it? Can you see repeating patterns of reaction in your own life? Can it liberate you from the depths of your soul? Can you acknowledge that your response is purely your ego's need to be right?

Most importantly, are you capable of listening to an opinion that differs from yours without feeling the need to shoot it down? Can you be comfortable with that opinion simply existing?

The following is my story and it needs to be told, even if only for me. It is my story of what happened to me, in Melbourne, during the pandemic. It is my story about the effects the pandemic had on me personally, physically, mentally and socially.

Everything I write about is from my experience and my perspective, and I'm honouring this. But I'm also giving you space to honour yours.

PART 1:

The Covid pandemic lockdown in Melbourne

There will be as many perspectives about the Covid lockdowns as there are people who experienced them. Who is to say that one perspective is more correct than another – it's a perspective.

And this is my perspective.

All I ask is that you keep an open mind because mine will probably be a perspective you were unaware of, mainly because it wasn't discussed in mainstream media.

Why?

Put simply, media organisations enforced government-directed health policies that required their staff to be vaccinated. To talk about this nationally in the media would be the same as organisations that actively championed this turning around and saying they were wrong. That's not going to happen. It would also take the government saying they were wrong.

In a society where we apparently teach people to learn from their mistakes, there is a big gaping silence on this front. And it needs to be talked about.

The significant dates

As with perspective, whether or not specific dates are 'significant' is relative. For context, however, in my circumstances, there were a number of very significant dates – the ones that impacted me personally and likely impacted a number of other people in similar situations in Melbourne.

Do any of these dates resonate with you? Or maybe you have your own list of dates that either threw you a curve ball or flicked you a lifeline. Can't remember the dates? I wouldn't be surprised given the number of times our government changed its mind and its stance on recommendations, closures and mandates. However, this same government now has a recorded history of what it said over those three-plus years. It's there for all to see and cannot be denied.

Let's take a look shall we?

Late 2020

- 19 August: (Former) Prime Minister Scott Morrison clarifies on radio 2GB "It is not going to be compulsory to have the vaccine, OK? It's not compulsory. There are no compulsory vaccines in Australia. There are no things that force people to do things."[2]

    Earlier in the day the PM told listeners of Neil Mitchell on 3AW he "would expect it to be as mandatory as you can possibly make."[3]

2021

- April: The World Health Organization cautioned that "if mandatory vaccination is considered necessary to interrupt transmission chains and prevent harm to others, there should be sufficient evidence that the vaccine is efficacious in preventing serious infection and/or transmission"[4]

- 24 May: Pfizer first available to under-50s
- 29 July: Brad Hazzard (former Minister for Health and Medical Research of New South Wales) stated, "There are a lot of people who don't base their decisions in science or evidence .... I'd say to those ... not wanting to take vaccines, my message to them is you're being extremely selfish if you think you can not have a vaccine just because you don't want to have a vaccine. Well, you should think about what you're doing to your family and to the community ..."[5]
- 18 August: vaccine numbers now added to the daily case numbers
- 23 August: (Former) Prime Minister Scott Morrison states, "Nationally we are aiming to live with Covid."[6]
- 31 August: Dan Andrews (former Premier of Victoria), discusses how the end of lockdown won't be based on vaccination rates but the ability to control a threshold of low Covid case numbers. He is aiming towards zero and a meeting later tonight will decide what low number of cases in the community will be acceptable to relax some of the harsh restrictions.[7]
- 5 September: Dan Andrews announced, "We're going to move to a situation where, to protect the health system, we're going to lock out people who are not vaccinated and can be. If you're making the choice not to get vaccinated, then you're making the wrong choice. And for safety's sake, back to that point of how much work our nurses have to do, as this becomes absolutely a pandemic of the unvaccinated, and we open everything up, it's not going to be safe for people who are not vaccinated to be roaming around the place spreading the virus. That's what they'll be doing."[8]

- 27 October: Unvaccinated people may enter retail stores but once the 90% target is reached, only vaccinated people will be allowed
- 29 October: businesses allowing access to unvaccinated people can be fined up to $500,000
- 19 November: (Former) Prime Minister Scott Morrison announces, "We're not in favour of mandatory vaccines imposed by the government."[9]

2022

- 10 January: (Serbian tennis player) Novak Djokovic is cleared to play in the Australian Open despite being unvaccinated
- 16 January: Djokovic ruling overturned and he is deported
- 27 January: In response to being questioned about the QR code system remaining in place to detect unvaccinated people (rather than its initial purpose of contact tracing), Dan Andrews said, "It's sad we've got to have all these elaborate systems to keep people out who have made the wrong choice. I wish people would just go and get vaccinated."[10]
- 28 March: Dan Andrews tests positive to Covid despite attending a function masked, while vaccinated and via a vaccinated economy
- 23 April: Unvaccinated people can now enter society but are still unable to work in many settings
- 19 June: mandate rules are lifted but individual organisations are allowed to set their own rules
- 11 October: Pfizer director admits vaccine was never tested on preventing transmission – which would make all the mandates illegal, as the World Health Organization stated in 2021[11]

2023

- 10 January: Hospitalisations for Covid in Australia no longer report whether people are vaccinated or not, as a report finds non-vaccinated people are not ending up in hospital
- 6 February: Dan Andrews announces, "Vaccines are now a feature of employment law, not mandates under the public health and wellbeing act, but there are some nationally consistent approaches for those who work in sensitive settings, for instance aged care workers and hospital workers."[12]
- 12 July: Workplaces are told to destroy information on Covid vaccinated staff
- 20 July: Unvaccinated mother, Vicki Derderian, is now crowd sourcing funds for a heart transplant overseas after losing a Victorian Civil and Administrative Tribunal (VCAT) appeal against The Alfred Hospital in Melbourne for refusing her a heart transplant on the grounds of Covid vaccination[13]
- 22 July: An article in *The Weekend Australian* newspaper reveals how banned Covid posts have now been deemed factual[14]
- 1 August: 16-year-old, unvaccinated girl, Dazelle Peters, is refused a double lung transplant by Sydney's St Vincent hospital due to vaccination status[15]
- 10 November: Covid cases now only reported on a monthly basis
- 31 December: Covid 19 vaccines are said to offer 'good protection' and mandates still remain for some industries

That's a long list, even without including everything. If you're confused, then you get my point. It was confusing. And frustrating. Everyone seemed to have their own agenda and their own information source, and nobody wanted to listen to anybody else.

The only thing I wish for is that the government apologise for the suffering they caused the unvaccinated population. The loss of jobs, the loss of livelihood and the ongoing, unnecessary segregation – just for the sake of not having to admit they were wrong.

Questions to ponder

Why are there even still mandates? Why do we treat unvaccinated people any differently when, apparently, after thirty days, your vaccine is no longer efficient anyway. Doesn't that mean that you're technically unvaccinated after this time, especially if you haven't kept up with your boosters?

Lockdown

On 20 March 2020, after two months of warning about the effects of Covid and public service announcements about how to keep yourself safe by limiting unnecessary movement, meticulous handwashing and social-distancing measures, Melbourne, the capital city of the state of Victoria in Australia, enforced the first stage of a lockdown and closed several businesses. On the 31st March, strict 'stay-at-home' orders were announced for its residents.

The basic facts

Over the next twenty months, Melbourne took the title of the most locked-down city in the world.

We were all divided into 'essential workers' and 'non-essential workers'. Initially, essential workers consisted of those internal and external people who were keeping supermarkets, doctors' offices, hospitals, nursing homes, emergency services, essential transport and the media running. Essential workers were exempt from stay-at-home restrictions but had to carry evidence that their outside journey was travelling to or from work and were often stopped by police checks. The rest of us – the non-essentials – stayed inside for twenty-three hours a day, working from home if we could, seeing family and friends only on Zoom or during a quick walk with only one other person, provided they lived within your five kilometres.

Five kilometres? Yes, this was as far from our homes as we were allowed to travel for 151 of those days before an increase was made to ten kilometres, and then to twenty-five kilometres.

If you were unlucky enough to live in one of the nine housing commission towers in North Melbourne and Flemington in July 2020, you might currently be part of the $5 million settlement the government had to pay for denying access to or from the buildings for up to fourteen days.[16] Before aid agencies stepped in, it initially meant up to 3000 vulnerable people were cut off from access to food and basic necessities, such as nappies and toiletries, until a safe way of providing basic needs was established.

For around half of the lockdown period, residents were permitted to spend one hour per day outside their home. This was considered 'exercise time' and, for a while, meant being in continual motion without being able to sit down on a park bench for a breather, and was only allowable within a five-kilometre radius of your residence. A raft of strict measures also saw public facilities – such as children's playgrounds and skate parks – taped off.

Masks were mandatory, both indoors and outdoors, for many of those days.

A curfew was put in place between 8 pm and 5 am, and, at 8:01 pm every night, a police helicopter would fly overhead to catch those still on the streets. It didn't matter if you were a 'fuck lockdown' vigilante, an asthma sufferer trying to take a breath outside their mask when walking up a hill or an 80-year-old grandpa taking a break on a park bench, anyone caught breaking the rules was fined for their breech. Protesters were arrested and the streets were filled with police as heavily armed as a riot squad.

Apart from the one-hour exercise allowance, people were only allowed to leave their home for a trip to the supermarket, doctor or pharmacist, or if they were providing care for a person who didn't live in their house.

The extreme nature of this Melbourne lockdown saw non-essential city workers confined to their homes for a minimum of 262 days over a two-year period.

For many of us, however, this period was longer due to different industries of business been forced to stagger their return to work. Plus, the government's decision on rules around social interactions meant that for 272 days we could not have visitors to our homes.

If, like me, you owned a fitness studio – each time, one of the first industries to close and one of the last to reopen – or worked as a driving instructor, lockdown lasted a total of around 350 days. That's nearly a year out of two years. Worse, if you were employed in tourism or large public venues, or if you were a musician or performer relying on the opening of those spaces, you clocked up around 400 days of being unable to work.

Lockdown broken down

For clarity, that 262-day record was not consecutive days, but blocks of time over a total of six lockdown periods between March 2020 and October 2021. I'm not sure whether consecutive days would have been worse, or better than the excitement of being 'let out', only to be confined again.

This is what the official 'stay-at-home' lockdown orders looked like for Melburnians:

- Lockdown 1: Tuesday 31 March 2020 to Tuesday 12 May 2020 (43 days)
- Lockdown 2: Thursday 9 July 2020 to Tuesday 27 October 2020 (111 days)
- Lockdown 3: Saturday 13 February 2021 to Wednesday 17 February 2021 (5 days)
- Lockdown 4: Friday 28 May 2021 to Thursday 10 June 2021 (14 days)
- Lockdown 5: Friday 16 July 2021 to Tuesday 27 July 2021 (12 days)
- Lockdown 6: Thursday 5 August 2021 to Thursday 21 October 2021 (77 days)

The lockdown inside the lockdown: the fitness industry

I specifically mentioned the fitness industry above as this is the industry most relevant to me, although others would have experienced the same. Basically, while the official number of locked-down days is reported as 262 – a globally-known world record – tallying actual days is somewhat trickier.

While some sites in the fitness industry may have recorded as many as 368 lockdown days, my own fitness business tallied up 338 days. That's around 11 months of being unable to open my commercial space and being closed to clients. In all honesty, mine may have been longer but it was so confusing by the end, I didn't know if I were Arthur or Martha.

Why the confusion?

Simply put, it was due to the sheer number of rules and regulations surrounding Melbourne's lockdown. We had lockdowns inside of lockdowns inside of lockdowns.

Businesses had a staggered approach to reopening, depending on the industry they were in and their ability to keep people safe. Owners of fitness studios and driving schools were among the very last ones to come out of lockdown each time. This is where I sat – one foot in the fitness industry, the other as a driving instructor.

The restrictions applied to driving schools were easy to understand – a very close proximity and a rotating door of clients. The only time I could teach people to drive in Melbourne was when every restriction was lifted and people were allowed to move around and do as they pleased.

A fitness business was a different kettle of fish. As a Pilates instructor, you could offer clinical Pilates at a private commercial business as an essential service – IF you were trained as a physio. Personal trainers were allowed to return to outdoor private sessions earlier than gyms were allowed to open. If you taught group sessions, you were also allowed to return to teaching outside classes slightly earlier than the gyms were allowed to open, but there were limits on capacity. If your studio was of a certain size, you could fit in a few people as per the 'four square metre' rule, so once venues were allowed to start reopening, it may have been financially viable for you to reopen with limited participation. If you didn't have the space, it was probably not worth reopening and was best to keep running classes outside.

But wait, there was more.

If you lived in a particular postcode at one period of time, you had an extra lockdown inside a lockdown and couldn't do any of the above. If you ran your business from a home address, and it fit within the later introduction of the 'two visitors per day to your property', you could probably swing opening slightly earlier. You may have also done personal training on the sly when you were allowed to 'exercise' outside with one friend in your allowable one hour of outside time. If you were a larger scale fitness business, you were still closed. If you were a sporting group, school sports clinic or a sports stadium, you were still closed.

It's confusing just writing about it. So, trying to tally the days was something I gave up on – it's not an exact science. Too many variables. And, in my defence, if you had survived 338 days with your way of life being locked down, you lived on your own with a five-kilometre radius rule, and your closest family was a two-hour drive away – you probably had no idea what was right or wrong by this stage. Hence, the discrepancy in the dates of fitness businesses being closed.

Forgive me.

The lockdown on top of the lockdown inside the lockdown: the unvaccinated

In addition to the lockdown of the general population in Melbourne, plus the lockdown of the fitness industry, we can add the lockdown of the unvaccinated. In numerical terms, simply add at least an extra 184 days on top of whichever lockdown already applied to you and your business.

What did this mean for me?

Over the 25-month period between March 2020 and April 2022, I spent around 522 days in lockdown. That is two days shy of doubling Melbourne's original world record of 262.

This number represents the total number of days I wasn't allowed to live a normal life based on my location, my profession – and my decision.

It is important to point out here that for some unvaccinated people, lockdown still hasn't ended to this day. If they work in what is deemed a high-risk setting – hospitals, emergency services, aged care facilities – and even government-run services like leisure centres – at the time of writing this book, there is still a vaccination requirement to adhere to.

The 184 days, therefore, is a sliding scale.

Greater Melbourne vs the rest of Victoria

During the Australia-wide lockdown – periods determined by each state government – there were considerable differences in conditions and lockdown periods. Naturally, this created angst and division between the states as Covid became more about politics and point-scoring than the population they represented and served.

Nowhere, however, was there a greater division than within Victoria and the Greater Melbourne area specifically. A city of 5 million people were essentially forced to be openly divided as they battled with the challenges of having to deal with harsh lockdown conditions. Thirty-one local government areas, including Mitchell Shire, were considered part of the Greater Melbourne area, and they rapidly became known as 'the Ring of Steel'. Any area outside the 'ring of steel' were considered regional Victoria.

The point of division came with the realisation that the 'ring of steel' and regional Victoria were not always under the same lockdown conditions. Regional areas had more freedom to move around, returned to work much earlier than Melburnians, did not face a nighttime curfew and moved in and out of lockdown depending on the Covid transmission numbers.

During the 262 days of Melbourne lockdown, most other states of Australia – and regional Victoria – had either completely reopened, had less restrictive conditions, had shorter periods of isolation, had barely experienced lockdown or had a 'hard border' so their own citizens could do as they pleased but no-one was allowed to enter or exit.

Reopening

As Melburnians neared the end of lockdown, a very clear goal was set in place, with certain – constantly changing – conditions needing to be met prior to reopening: over ninety-five per cent of the eligible population were to be vaccinated in Victoria. Eligible referred to 'anyone over the age of sixteen and without a medical exemption'. I am yet to meet one person who qualified for an exemption.

The government determined a deadline for vaccination, stating that people who wanted to be part of society would need to have their first dose before 15 October 2021, and their second before 26 November 2021. They would still be refused entry into places until they were fully vaccinated but would be able to work – provided they were booked to be vaccinated prior to the second dose cut-off. Different industries, like construction and emergency services, had earlier dates mandated for their second dose.

The 'vaccinated economy'

Between the reopening on 21 October 2021, and 22 April 2022, Melburnians were required to show their vaccination status in order to gain entry to most public spaces. This became referred to as the 'vaccinated economy'.

Country Victoria, who'd already reopened, trialled the vaccinated economy concept from 11 October 2021, prior to Melburnians being allowed out of lockdown. The trial involved unvaccinated people being refused entry into businesses other than supermarkets and other essential services, such as petrol stations and doctors.

When the government reopened most areas in Melbourne on October 21, the majority of businesses started checking vaccination certificates – even though they were not yet mandated to do so. At this time, my own business was still closed and I remember getting my Christmas shopping done in carefully selected places during the first week of November, just before the vaccinated economy trial was declared successful and slated for implementation Victoria-wide.

What not being vaccinated meant for those like me was that we weren't allowed out in public for a further six months. You may feel this is justified in high-risk spaces, like hospitals and nursing homes. You might even agree that not being allowed to go shopping at Kmart or have a pub meal was par for the course. However, during that period of time a few other rules were enacted in the name of protecting the general public from the unvaccinated. We could not attend housing inspections to purchase or rent a property. We were not allowed to step inside school grounds to drop children off or attend assemblies and sports days. In some cases, individual schools took it upon themselves to even ban unvaccinated primary and secondary school students from these events. And many people weren't even afforded the right to step foot in their workplace and had their jobs terminated – despite the fact they were successfully working from home – with employers citing noncompliance.

On 16 December 2021, heading into Christmas, an announcement regarding group sizes at gatherings was made, with strict regulations should your group include unvaccinated people. Interstate travel was not allowed from 5 November if you were not vaccinated. And, from 27 November, any international arrivals who were unvaccinated had to quarantine for fourteen days before being allowed to enter Melbourne.

Read that previous sentence again.

An unvaccinated person from another country was allowed to land here, do their quarantine and then enter Melbourne. Yet, as an unvaccinated citizen of Australia, I was restricted from leaving the state, walking into many shops and businesses, operating my business and seeing too many people from my family for Christmas.

The apparent end of the vaccine mandate

It wasn't until 23 April 2022 that the government stopped the vaccinated economy and allowed people to move freely around Melbourne without having to prove their status.

And it wasn't until 25 June 2022 that they dropped the vaccine mandate for workers in a large number of industries.

This was meant to be a time of realisation and gratitude – knowing that, as hard as it was to hold out, you had finally made it.

It was anything but.

With its policy on the way out, the government then decided to add one final blow – continuation of the vaccination status for employment or participation would be up to the individual organisations themselves.

And this is where it got nasty.

This is when people showed their true colours.

The government-mandated rules we'd lived by for so long had given me a sense of security that people were only acting the way they were because they were scared at the time, because they were told to, and because they had no choice. At least, that's what I allowed myself to believe because it was easier to deal with.

How wrong could I have been?

This new 'freedom' brought about months of free-range decisions regarding what individuals thought was right or wrong. Seeing what people truly felt about me and my decision was an eye-opening experience. Emotionally, it was probably the hardest to deal with in the whole shit show.

While we were living by 'the rules', it had been easy for me to work out where I could and couldn't go. It was easy for me to choose not to participate socially because I simply knew I wouldn't be allowed in most places. In regard to driving lessons and tests, I knew the rules of my workplace. I knew I couldn't run a Pilates business or work as a Pilates instructor until that time.

For a short time, I wrongly believed all of that had ended, but giving businesses and organisations the ability to choose if they wanted to continue to discriminate was the kicker none of us expected. And, by this stage, everyone was so vitriolic about their right to treat you like shit because you weren't one of them; you weren't someone willing to protect their fellow man.

I had to fight for my right to continue to sit in on the driving tests of my students as new rules about showing a negative Rapid Antigen

Test (RAT) test before participation came in and a great percentage of testing officers at VicRoads expressed that they were not happy about having me in the car. My poor students, who had done all their driving and gathered their skills, and were trying to stay calm for the test, also had to deal with officers threatening to not take them because I was in the car. I had to liaise with the person in charge. I had to attend a meeting. I had to listen to my public shaming between a manager and a testing officer when they thought I had already walked out of the building. I had to detail my treatment in an email more than once just so those testing officers could be taught that I was not breaking any rules and was adhering to a policy they created; and they didn't get to decide whether they liked it or not.

During this period, I also tried to apply for jobs teaching Pilates and yoga, not knowing whether I would have to show a passport I didn't have. I tried at a few leisure centres first, but because they were government-run, I needed proof of vaccination status. I also was in desperate need of a holiday and went to a flight centre, only to be told that the majority of the places I wanted to travel to wouldn't let 'someone like me' in. These moments occurred after my 522 days of penance.

It wasn't until June 2023 that the government requested organisations destroy Covid vaccine information and personal data collected on people.

Fourteen months on from the end of the vaccinated economy.

In that fourteen months, I lost friends who didn't want me to come back around. I distanced myself from extended family members who were clearly still ashamed of and by me. I maintained a few friendships with people who seemed to want to only meet me outside in a public setting.

Knowing that people are scared of you after the amount of time you have been in their life hurts more than you can imagine.

A quick summary

That record number of 262 days in lockdown ended in late October 2021. Staggered business returns happened between then and January 2022. Unvaccinated people were only allowed to move more freely around from late April 2022, yet workplace mandates continued to be enforced in a majority of organisations until June 2023. It may just look like a series of dates – a slow progression – but what it meant was that a large majority of businesses were allowed to continue to hire on the basis of vaccination status twenty months after the lockdown officially ended. If you were unvaccinated and worked in an industry closed during the whole pandemic period then you have been unable to operate as a functioning working member of society for almost three-and-a-half years.

Let me tell you – that lack of purpose deeply affects a person.

So … June 2023. The real date of normalcy for me – but not for those who work in a high-risk area or want an organ transplant. Sadly, it still continues.

Ongoing restrictions

Despite the Victorian Government denouncing the need to ask for vaccination status in June 2023 and requesting businesses to destroy private records on their staff and any collected on patrons, many job ads to this very day (10 September 2023), documents requiring health details, visa applications for travel and the like still contain questions pertaining to a person's need to be vaccinated. Having recently applied for a job, I know you still can't work for a local council leisure centre without showing proof of your vaccination status.

Restrictions still remain for those working in health and aged care in Victoria and the same goes for some in-patient services. At the time of writing, life-saving and elective surgeries can still be dismissed on the basis of vaccination status.

This does not only apply to Melbourne. In Queensland, they waited until September 2023 to drop the requirement for health care workers to be fully vaccinated and are still making their way through ongoing dispute settlements on a case-by-case basis for the people whose jobs they terminated and can now legally reinstate. A recent news report discussed whether those returning would be subject to a penalty on their record for originally refusing vaccination.

Many of those who chose not to get vaccinated had careers in industries where they served the community. Some had built their whole life around helping others but, because of the choice they made, were forced to walk away from who they were. In many cases, this was a choice they stuck with, despite constant harassment and abuse, all while dealing with their own dark thoughts and imposter syndrome. While many were steadfast, honest and committed to their decision, the narrative around vaccinations was able to gradually change – but not the rules associated with them.

Initially, we were all informed that this vaccine would not only stop people from catching Covid but also prevent it being passed on. But look at the progression – the vaccine went from being the only thing that was going to stop the spread, to something that would lessen your chance of getting Covid, or at least stop it from being as severe, and finally to something that merely offered 'good' protection. Those of us who made the choice not to have it never wavered in our strength of conviction – despite losing employment, housing and relationships. The supporters of the vaccine also stuck to their original beliefs in its benefits, to the point where that 'good' protection was still a strong enough reason to lock the unvaccinated out of society.

Our 'choice' left many without money, without a sense of purpose and with a societal division so deep, friends and family were convinced they had a right to no longer trust people they had known their whole lives.

It's interesting that the people who made a decision and stuck to it despite all outside pressure and internal stress ended up being the ones seen as crazy, unreliable, weak, dangerous and selfish. They were seen to have a blatant disregard for science, safety and authority. Questionable people. Liars who had no worth here.

On the other side, the ones who kept changing the narrative and presenting different facts each month became the heroes, worshipped for their efforts, and the only people worth listening to.

I'm here to change that. Because that narrative is wrong.

PART 2:

My story

We all have a brain and we are all capable of using it to decide what is right and wrong. The most important task of our brain, however, is to understand the large spectrum between those two extremes. Under stress, our brains struggle to accept the middle ground. We want one answer, one person responsible, one justified reaction, one outcome. Training our brains to listen, process and ask questions, and then respond respectfully, is difficult. It's a skill that takes time and a lot of practice, but eventually, it rewards us. It makes us more curious about the world, reminds us we're alive and surrounded by others who are also learning the hard lessons of this journey.

My brain definitely reminds me I'm alive, often in the most excruciating of ways. At times, it's made me wish I wasn't.

Living with Trigeminal neuralgia

I was medically diagnosed with Trigeminal neuralgia (TN) in early 2009. Feel free to Google it – you'll likely discover it's referred to as 'The Suicide Disease'. TN is known to be the second most painful condition you could possibly experience – 44 on the McGill Pain Scale – only just behind complex regional pain syndrome, which sits at forty-six. If you think about giving birth or severing a limb, TN is more painful – not that I've done either of those; it's an example for context. The American Association of Neurological Surgeons classifies the condition in the following way:

> *Trigeminal neuralgia (TN), also known as tic douloureux, is sometimes described as the most excruciating pain known to humanity. ... This intense, stabbing, electric shock-like pain is caused by irritation of the trigeminal nerve, which sends branches to the forehead, cheek and lower jaw.*

I was diagnosed at 26 years of age, after a few months of putting up with what I thought was tooth pain. Each visit to the dentist became worse. I was halfway through a root canal when the pain went through the roof. I couldn't deal with it anymore. I was referred to a specialist and prescribed an anti-convulsant to see if it was the equivalent of my lower jaw having a variety of seizures. The medication eased the pain, so it was decided a trip to the neurologist was in order. From the first time I noted the pain, through various dental appointments, visits to specialists and scans, and on to my final appointment with my neurologist Dr Hilary Hunt, it took around six months to diagnose it. This timeline is extremely quick for some sufferers, many of whom can take years to find out.

Why did it start? Who knows? At the end, two years later, the majority of the pain was found to be caused by an enlarged blood vessel that became trapped and physically wrapped around the nerve. Was that the cause initially? Possibly but three MRIs didn't pick it up and, honestly, I don't think anyone will ever know. Did it also begin within the same year as another heavily advocated vaccine of which I took three doses before the free trial ended for women aged under twenty-six? I'll leave you to decide but it was worth mentioning in the full timeline of my story.

At the end of the day, I don't know what caused it but I have my theories and I wouldn't be giving an honest account of my feelings towards all of this if I didn't mention it. I also later discovered there have been concerns voiced about it being linked to other neuro conditions. Did I find this information via a reputable source? If you consider the Cancer Council of Australia as reputable, then yes.

In a nutshell, TN presents as nerve pain in your face – either the jaw, eye, nose, mouth or forehead, depending on which of the five branches the pain originates from. If you're incredibly unlucky, you'll have more than one. You can't eat properly. At times, you can't talk properly. Forget about going outside if the breeze is cold. It can be a task to brush your teeth, blink, smile or do any number of basic functions on any given day.

I went through periods of not getting out of bed for days, not being able to eat, not being able to talk and, the most damaging of all, trying my best to both ignore and hide the excruciating pain I was in from everyone else – friends, work colleagues and the general public. At my worst, I moved away from everyone I knew in Melbourne and hid in Ballarat, a large country town about ninety mins out of the city.

At the time, I was working in my first, and only, full-time job, in a commercial television newsroom. It was here that I was exposed to the pressure and unfairness of the world. At the age of twenty-one, my introduction to video editing was to watch the footage that came in from war zones across the world and edit around the bits that were too gruesome to show on television. Before everyone had an iPhone and became their own newscaster, that type of sensitivity to what the general public saw was paramount. We took out the death, the blood and anything that looked like a body part, then pieced together a 30-second story showing pictures of building destruction and people crying.

You never knew what you were going to be sent from an international newsfeed. If it was a local feed, like a car accident or a bushfire, the camera operators were the ones who faced the horrors and shot around them. They never exposed the editors and producers to what they had seen and for that I am grateful.

During my six years in a newsroom, I edited pieces on the Kerang train crash, the hit-and-run of six teenagers in Mildura, multiple gangland killings and the Black Saturday bushfires. It can desensitise you, especially when you are against the clock, trying to create something that wins the nightly news viewership. You start to think in terms of 'Who did they interview?' and 'Why didn't we get that shot?' instead of 'I hope these people are okay' and 'Is anyone offering them help? I believe the team dealt with it almost collectively without ever really expressing it. We had our Friday night drinks, we had our massive boozy events, we breathed down each others' necks and pushed the boundaries of fair work treatment, just to get stuff done. Dealing with the pressure was a badge of honour. And it was exciting because you felt like you were part of something. The 4 am starts and working six Christmas days in a row were just par for the course.

I loved it – until I found sport.

What followed over my next nine years was less of the heavy content but more of the pressure and excitement of a live television sports broadcast. I basically followed the sports seasons around. January was the Australian Open, February was often a mix of random projects until the AFLW came into play, March to October was the AFL season, November was the horseracing and December to January was the Big Bash cricket. These major events were my bread-and-butter, with a little NBL, cycling, A-league, a few panel shows and a long-form documentary or two thrown in to round out the year. I travelled around Australia and overseas to the venues. I ran thousands of replays of marks and goals, big hits and classic catches, hooves in the grass at slowmo speed. I pressed play on sponsored segments, competitions and celebrities in a marquee. I spent hours in hire cars, at airports and in hotel rooms before returning home to re-edit my work again for continued analysis throughout the week regarding who to watch and how that team or individual got the chocolates.

Sometimes, I edited amazing colour pieces to music and visual effects. Sometimes, I had 30 seconds to slab together the last four times a player touched the ball. Sometimes, I had 3 seconds to cue up what just happened. Sometimes, I produced the order of replay sequences. Sometimes, I spent a week carefully telling the story of a legend in their sport. Sometimes, I spent three months piecing together a documentary with multiple interviews, various pieces of vision and audio from a variety of sources.

What I never had was time. Not just the time to get things to air because of deadlines but time to myself. Time to think. Time to process. Time to enjoy the simple things in life. Time to think about who I was, what I wanted and where I was headed. Time to listen to whether my body wanted to keep up with the pace of my mind.

And everything was fast-paced. I walked fast, I talked fast, I drove fast. I often had zero patience. I scheduled my friends into the small windows of time available to me. I scheduled too many things in a day. I multitasked to the extreme. I failed to slow down when needed, and when forced to, I realised I didn't know how.

There is a constant level of tension in the air when you work in a deadline industry – and it consumes your life. Unless you are great at disassociating, which I never was, it follows you around like a bad smell, dictating who you are in your day-to-day dealings. The pressure I felt to perform each working day carried through in my private life. Calm was almost the scariest thing I would ever have to be. There had to be an edge to everything. It was both exhausting and motivating.

I didn't have the concentration for silence and meditation. I didn't have the patience for people who didn't know what they were doing. I didn't have the appreciation for the beauty in each day. And I definitely did not have time to listen to the warning signs my body was sending out that all was not right in my world.

For a sufferer of TN, there are days when it feels like there will be no end to the pain – except the obvious. I had thought about it several times. Working in Melbourne while living in Ballarat, I distinctly remember a particularly difficult morning. I was on an extraordinarily large dose of anti-convulsant medication, so much so that it gave me the shakes and blurred vision for about 90 minutes after I'd taken it. I developed a routine where I'd set an alarm for 4 am, roll over, take my meds and go back to sleep until 6 am. The tablets sat on the bedside table on top of a piece of paper on which I'd written a quote during another hard day of my illness.

> ***Throw it all at me, take everything you can,***
> ***even in the end I will not be defeated.***

This quote was my reminder that the most important thing each day was to just get up and keep going. If I had my time again, however, I would approach it differently. I'd have a quote to remind me to ask for help, rather than try to outrun my illness.

This particular morning, I couldn't fall back asleep and eventually succumbed to getting up to use the bathroom. It was 4:30 am. I never made it. I collapsed halfway up the hallway as I couldn't walk in a straight line and had no idea where I was actually going. I lay on the floor in tears for half an hour until my housemate found me and helped me up. Embarrassed, I staggered to the bathroom, then struggled back down the hallway to my room, holding on to the wall.

"Are you okay?", he kept asking.

Ever stubborn, I replied I was fine. He'd been living with me for a few months but had no idea I was even unwell. Another time, he'd already left for work, and I'd woken and readied myself on that second alarm with the sudden thought – I reckon I'm done. I fully believed I was no longer able to convince the world I was fine and I'd rather just not be here. I got ready for work and left for the 1.5-hour drive into Melbourne, having decided it was my last day. That was it, I'd had enough.

How to do it, though? I couldn't take an excess of medication because it already wasn't getting rid of the pain, so it was unlikely to do greater than that. I drove past an area known as Anthony's Cutting. In 2010, it was a long drop down into a valley, with a speed limit of 110 km/h, and a steep incline back up a curvy hill, at a recommended 80 km. As I came down the hill that morning, I eyed the body of water at the bottom to the left. As it happened, I was having a painful seizure in my face at that exact moment. I checked around me – no-one in front or behind. I put my foot on the accelerator, closed my eyes and let go of the steering wheel.

I think back to this moment, mostly when I hear about someone who has taken their own life. My first thought is always that death wasn't their first intention – relieving themselves of pain was.

It's a weird juxtaposition; being in so much pain that you are begging for it to stop, and knowing your response won't only get rid of the pain, but will get rid of everything. It's a cry for help to make things better, while not fully appreciating that it means you won't get help because you'll no longer be here to receive it. It's a moment where you would literally do anything at all to feel something different – so much so you'd give up the ability to even exist and feel at all. It's a moment where the thought that 'anything is better than this' enters your mind, but the irony is that anything and nothing are not the same.

I honestly can't tell you what happened in that moment when I let go of the steering wheel. I wish I had a dashcam to figure it out. I remember thinking it should be over by now, but when I opened my eyes, I saw I'd somehow made it almost to the top of the curvy hill – without veering off course. It should've been impossible without steering and I don't believe I'd ever be able to recreate it if I tried. Call it divine intervention, call it luck, call it whatever you will – it wasn't my time.

I remember contacting a friend that evening. "I'm not coping," I said. I knew I needed to be a little more forthright in explaining this to people.

But I never had the chance because, only a handful of weeks later, I found myself at the crossroads between life and death again.

On 14 Dec 2010, I was supposed to be going to Perth to produce the big-screen content for The Ashes. Nothing out of the ordinary, except I'd already travelled quite extensively in the last month, a variety of flights at all hours of the day. I'd been at the grounds as early as 5 am to witness anthem dress rehearsals and late finishes, with debrief meetings in the hotel after a full day of cricket. I hadn't slept much and was on an extremely high dose of medication to not feel any pain.

I'd just come out of eight months of AFL and the only week I had free to chill, between cricket and footy, was taken away by the fact that Collingwood and St Kilda drew their first Grand Final and had to replay it the following week.

Christmas was coming and, in addition to keeping up with work events, I wanted to be a normal, socialising human. With so much going on, I'd missed a few doses of medication. As the producer, everyone at work was relying on me telling them what to do, and I believed I couldn't show any weakness. I was a female working in sport; I had no time to listen to what my body – and my neurologist – wanted, which was to be in hospital on morphine. I only had time to prove I wouldn't let anyone down and that I could do what they were paying me for. The thing was, I physically couldn't. My mouth was seizing and I couldn't talk. My brain was pulsing and I couldn't think.

Before I could get on that plane to Perth, I had to get to the chemist. I needed that medication. Opening my car door, I was about to step in when I had a massive seizure and ended up on the floor of my garage. Luckily, my phone was in my pocket. With some presence of mind, I rang an ambulance, but they couldn't understand me. My mouth was contorted, making speaking impossible. Instead, I rang my cousin, who didn't need to understand me; she just knew where to come. She'd been standing in a queue for almost an hour, waiting to get a photo with Santa, but she understood the urgency and sacrificed her place. When she arrived, she yelled out to me. She was knocking on the door and the windows. The two children – her daughter and a friend - were still in her car. Noisy and agitated, they were matching the energy of the intense situation.

I could hear her but she couldn't find me up the steep hill of my driveway. I was too far away from the front door and I couldn't yell out. Laying in my garage, I managed to drag myself back to the open car door. I reached up and bashed the horn over and over and over.

At the entrance to the emergency department of Ballarat Base Hospital, I dragged myself out of her car – my cousin had to find a park and get the children out of their seats in the back. Somehow, I managed to get myself inside.

My story

"Morphine," I screamed. "Morphine." It was the only word I had the energy to say.

I don't know if you've ever struggled into an emergency department on your own, looking high as a kite on exceptionally large doses of prescribed pain medication, with no sleep, unstable on your feet, barely dressed in anything that makes sense, and screaming for morphine out of a contorted mouth like your life depends on it. It's not well-received. I certainly didn't look like your average Ballarat homeowner with a successful career in television, who was just trying to get some assistance with pain management for a neurological condition no-one had ever heard of.

No. I looked like a junkie who'd just come off the street. And for the first two hours after I'd arrived, that's exactly how I was treated. It's no surprise really, because I was literally screaming and pleading more than I ever have for someone to help me, and simultaneously wanting to be physically dead. If there had been anything useful in reach, I would've ended it right there.

While I was waiting for my cousin, so she could speak on my behalf, I tried texting my condition on my phone and showing it to the woman fronting triage. She wouldn't look and just pushed forms at me. "Go and sit down and fill these in," she said. "Then we can see about having someone help you."

When I finally saw someone, they had to Google my condition. Only then was I put in a wheelchair and taken through to emergency. I was still alone as they wouldn't let my cousin, with her double pram, into the emergency bays because she wouldn't fit. My only option was to continue using my mobile to explain my situation.

My relief at seeing a doctor come in was short-lived. He refused to communicate with me; refused to look at the information I was typing onto my phone telling him not to touch my face. I can only put it down to his ego. How dare I tell him how to assess a patient in his emergency department? Muttering something about lockjaw, he grabbed my face – and I struck him. "I won't treat this patient," he said.

So I was left there. In more pain. Agitated. Unable to explain my situation. No help.

Eventually, there was a shift change. The Associate Nurse Unit Manager stepped in, apparently wanting to know why there was someone screaming in an emergency bay at the top of her lungs. This beautiful angel was the only person in the whole emergency department that knew what TN was. "Put her on morphine, now," she demanded. All of a sudden, they were listening to my cries to get my neurologist on the phone to confirm my story.

Dr Hunt issued instructions for me to be transferred to the Epworth Hospital in Melbourne, and gave permission for me to be dosed up on an incredibly high level of morphine.

So high was the level of morphine that the patient transport people kept checking on me every ten minutes throughout the 90-minute journey, assuming I'd be put to sleep. I remember one saying, "Oh, you're still awake, honey. You've taken enough to put an elephant to sleep." After about the third check, where I still knew my name and how many fingers she was holding up, she become concerned with how alert I was, and started ringing other hospitals between Ballarat and Melbourne. "We don't have morphine on board," I heard her say, "and I'm worried she's going to need more."

Even with everything going on, I hadn't processed the seriousness of my situation until I arrived at Epworth and saw Dr Hunt standing at the end of the transport vehicle when the doors opened. There's nothing that screams 'serious' quite like a neurologist, who you have to book six months in advance for an appointment, actually making the time to meet you when you arrive at the hospital. To this day, she still tells me I was a special case. I hope, for her sake, she's not had another quite like it.

Every day for the next seven days, Dr Hunt came in to tell me I needed brain surgery. She even sent the surgeon in twice. For the first five days, I refused. I couldn't fathom being in any more pain and to hear the word 'surgery' and know they wanted to slice into my skull made no sense.

"I'm fine," I said, over and over.

"It's the morphine," she explained. "You'll either have to do the surgery or live in the hospital for the rest of your life."

Still, even after hearing her say that, I was convinced I could ween off it over time. She lowered my dose that evening and by the morning, I was screaming for the surgeon to come back. I agreed to the surgery and it was scheduled for the next day.

I remember requesting a last MRI before they cut open my skull so they could prove where they were taking the pain from. However, it didn't allay my fears as the results came back still inconclusive as to the trigger. I had no faith in the surgery. They still didn't know what was causing the pain, and I didn't want them to go in and cut me up, yet still not be able to find it. I was worried I'd be in worse pain than I already was. There was no underlying cause, not even in the hours before the surgery.

As they wheeled me into the operating theatre, I was still screaming in pain. My mother was holding my hand, and both of us were crying as the anaesthetist put me to sleep. All I had was the hope that they found something.

Luckily they did.

An enlarged blood vessel was not only pressing on the nerve – a common occurrence with TN – but it had pressed, wrapped around and then coated the nerve. This was why the pain was so intense and wasn't disappearing; the blood vessel was latched on and was like a switch unable to be turned off. It was also not visible on the MRI.

In a procedure known as microvascular decompression surgery, they separated the nerve from the blood vessel, put a whole heap of gauze in the side of my head to keep them apart, returned the drained brain fluid, screwed my skull back together and then stitched me back up like new.

I had the worst night's sleep. Unable to move my position in bed, I also had no control of the muscles in my head and neck and my brain felt like it was a shaken-up can of soft drink. To top it off, my parents came in briefly, holding a prawn pizza they'd tried to scoff for their dinner. The smell made me throw up violently for the next twelve hours. But, I couldn't complain – I was the lucky one. Diagnosed within six months of the first pain. Heavily medicated for just 18 months. Only one emergency department admission – admittedly the one that was very scary and resulted in invasive brain surgery.

Three days later, on Christmas Eve, I left the hospital. By mid-January, I'd returned to work, initially on limited duties. Then, six weeks after I'd returned, I was back to my normal workload; it was footy season after all, and that was my bread-and-butter. I figured I'd better show I was still capable and wouldn't let one month of inconvenience stop me.

What was I thinking?

The thing is, I wasn't thinking. I didn't process what had happened. My mindset was 'That happened to me. Life was shit. It's over now. We move on. Nothing to see here.' Not once did I look at that experience as a wake-up call. Not once did I realise it was an alarm going off in my body to tell me I needed to slow down. That I needed to focus on how I got there. That I needed to give myself a break. I just saw it as something unfortunate that happened and something I wasn't ever going to have to worry about again. Returning to work meant I didn't have to process it. Plus, I needed to make money again because, as a freelancer, it had been quite inconvenient to be without work for just over a month.

Not once did I stop and think: I've just had my skull drilled into, the contents of my brain shaken up and padding placed on the inside of my head. Instead, I expected to just pick up where I left off. Of course, I attended to the physical limitations – the neck pain, the slack muscles down the right side of my body that needed weekly clinical Pilates and massage. But, not once did I seek treatment for the psychological effects on my brain, let alone the trauma of that emergency department visit.

Those psychological effects – the process afterwards – are not talked about though. I had this belief that once it was done, that was it; I'd be cured and after rehab I'd be ready to return to my life as normal.

But that wasn't the case. I attempted it. I stuck at the attempt for a further eight years. But I've never felt the same since. Something in me had changed. I know the exact moment this happened – and it wasn't straight after the surgery.

There's a bi-annual retreat for sufferers of TN – and it's here that I had my forced epiphany. I was attending with my best friend, who I'd known since I was 12 years old. She was a nurse now and had decided to accompany me to the retreat in the Hunter Valley (NSW) in August of 2011. She thought she was there as a medical professional who could gain further understanding to help other TN patients she may meet in the future, while I believed I was attending to show there is light at the end of the tunnel, you just need the surgery first.

As part of the retreat, we all had the opportunity to share our stories. We weren't in a group full of sufferers who had never had relief – although those people did exist on this retreat – we were with people who were either in a period of relief after their second, third or even fifth surgery, and people who had tried various procedures and surgeries over the years and were lucky if they ever had up to a year's relief.

My friend and I were the last two people in the circle to speak. With each of the fifteen people having their say, my mood became lower and lower. I'd planned to say how lucky I was that I'd had my surgery in December, and how well it had obviously worked because it was now August and I was still pain free. But the stories I heard were: "I had my surgery in 2005 and it came back worse in 2006," or "I've had four surgeries now; the first one lasted three years, the rest less and less," and so on.

I was also judging the ages of these people as we went around the group – they were mostly twenty or more years older than me – some at least forty years older. With each story, my mind was frantic, screaming 'How many reoccurrences am I likely to experience if I live to 100?'

When it was my turn to share, I only managed to say, "My name is Lauren. I had surgery in December last year ..." Then, I couldn't say anything because I was overwhelmed by the patronising sighs and stares I felt from this room full of people who were now feeling sorry for me. People who were now seeing me as someone still coming to terms with what was to come.

When the moderator realised I couldn't finish, they moved on to my friend. "I don't think Lauren can go through all of this again," she managed through her tears. She was right. After all, she was the friend who answered the phone after the 'incident' at Anthony's Cutting.

There we sat. Me, frozen in silence, and my friend flooded with tears. Both of us drowning at the same time in the realisation – there is no cure for TN. You are simply in remission or you're not – and when you're not, the odds of it coming back with a vengeance are high.

When we left the group, we went back to our room before mealtime. I couldn't talk about what had just transpired. She couldn't fathom the information. We were both visibly floored and upset – just in different ways.

We nearly didn't go to dinner but I forced myself. I'm glad I did because that night I met an elderly American woman named Claire, who, if my memory serves me correctly, was the founder of the Facial Pain Association in the USA.

"I've been pain free for twenty-four years," she told me that night. "Don't listen to the stories. Go out and live your life the best you can. If it's going to happen again, you can't change that." She told me she'd made the decision, after her first surgery, to live a life she enjoyed, but also one that was healthy for her mind and body. "I don't sweat the small stuff," she added, "and I'm grateful for everything I have."

For Claire, it hasn't returned so far – but she doesn't even think about it like that. She doesn't count the weeks, months and years. She just lives truly and honestly, in the best way she can. "Who knows," she said, "I may equally get hit by a truck."

I've never seen Claire since that night, but she had such a profound impact on me I've never forgotten her. My new motto, right from that moment, was 'I'm going to be another Claire'. I find it a little poetic because, as a child, I used to dress up in a costume and a curly wig and ask to be called 'Claire-abelle'. I wouldn't answer to anything else. It was almost as if, in my child-like innocence, I already knew who 'future me' was.

Once I'd returned to Melbourne after the retreat, I asked about studying for a Pilates diploma when I attended my next clinical Pilates session. I'd decided that, like Claire, I was going to live a life that was healthier for my mind and body. For the next two years, while still working in TV, I studied to become a fully qualified Pilates professional. After I graduated, I continued with my TV job, as well as teaching Pilates, until I finally believed I was ready, and able, to leave for good in 2018.

Over the next twelve years, I learned that it took more than physical change to transition to a healthier, happier lifestyle. Removing myself from a stressful job, prioritising eating well and getting more exercise were all important, but a long-term change involved making time to listen to my mind and body, hear what they were trying to tell me and giving them what they needed. It also meant forgiving myself for my past mistakes, forgiving others for their misguided judgements, accepting I was human and embracing all my amazing flaws. It involved questioning my strongly held beliefs and really listening to others to find commonality rather than difference. It meant finding that passion for further study of interests that at first made no sense to me, and understanding I'm merely a student of life and there's always something to learn. Above all, it was about accepting that everything in life is connected and we all need to find what truly makes us who we are so our own cog in the wheel can spin harmoniously beside each and every other person in this world, with the ultimate goal that all people truly experience peace within themselves one day.

I've been in remission for all but three days for the last thirteen years.

That emergency department visit in 2010 stored itself in my body as trauma. I'm aware of it. I've given it time to process. I've learned to deal with it. I've honoured its existence and learned to change the way I think about it. It's taken time, both on my own with my thoughts and occasionally with the aid of professional help. This trauma has mostly shifted out of my body but it still has small triggers that I can now recognise when they present, and I can see the coping mechanisms start to take over. Some days are not as easy as others and that has a lot to do with where my mind is and how I'm best placed to deal with the situation. Mostly it revolves around how I've best shown up for myself that day. Am I wasting time being angry or have I fostered a beautiful relationship with the fact that I'm human?

And sometimes the human me has a bad day.

I can stand here and proudly say "I'm a survivor" rather than a sufferer out loud, knowing that it took a combination of two years of Cognitive Behavioural Therapy, the in-depth study of mindfulness, meditation and other trauma-healing practices and a shit-load of small physical adjustments in my life to finally change the narrative around my story.

It wasn't easy but I'm glad I did the work so I can fully move on from this part of my life in a positive way.

And it all started from journaling.

My story

Your turn

What is a part of your story that you rarely talk about but need to tell? Take your time and write about it here. Come back to it every so often to reread it, or add to it.

The Four Per Cent

When Covid hit

Australia's first reported case of Covid was on 25 January 2020 – in Melbourne. By mid-March, a state of emergency had been announced by the Victorian Government, and the first bans were put in place. Then, by the end of March, Melburnians were in lockdown.

The writing had been on the wall for several months and, being a close observer of such matters, I'd moved my business out of its first location the day before the lockdown was announced. At the time, it felt like I'd been the only person who knew this situation was going to be with us for quite some time.

I'm the type of person who actively evaluates everything before I make a decision, especially when it comes to my health. When our first lockdown started, I followed the rules, but was open-mindedly observing what was going on, trying to figure out what benefits the restrictions could have.

Although I'd done what was asked – shutting the doors of my business and begrudgingly remaining at home to 'stay safe' – I didn't agree with lockdown. For me, the number one way to actually lower a person's immunity is to isolate them, and then prevent them from participating in immune-boosting activities like being out in nature, socialising, exercising, and simply contributing to society. The constant cycle of fear also didn't help and I found myself wondering what made those in 'power' think that a continuous 'flashing red emergency ad break' telling us about all the things we couldn't do would possibly be more helpful than arming the community with information about what they could do to help themselves, and still be part of society.

Stay-at-home orders were lifted on 12 May 2020 but it wasn't until the end of June that restrictions were eased to the extent that I could reopen my business. Even then, I was cautious and waited for a week after I was technically allowed to reopen, which I did somewhat hesitantly in a different space.

As it turned out, I was right to be hesitant. It lasted a week before we were ordered to shut our doors again. While I'd suspected it for months, the order to close businesses again was when I knew for sure that this was going to continue for a long time.

I put my house up for sale, which unfortunately coincided with the introduction of ridiculously strict stage 4 restrictions that involved curfews, surveillance helicopters and strict lockdown laws that governed every movement – one part included real estate inspections not being allowed. Eventually, my house sold in December, five months after I'd listed it on the market!

It's funny how your mind draws connections, but the sale of my house somehow coincides in my memory with the initial discussions about vaccinations. I already knew I wouldn't be participating in any vaccination program and, at the start of 2021 when the idea of a vaccine mandate was being thrown around, I resolved to not succumb to any pressure.

There was some talk, with the belief from some corners, that a vaccination 'couldn't be forced' but I found that notion absurd. After all, hadn't these same people just experienced the curfews and the helicopters. Forcing people to be vaccinated was relatively minor by comparison. So, I knew there would be pressure – but I wasn't prepared for the actual extent of the pressure and, to be honest, I don't know how I survived it.

But, the fact was, I'd do anything to not end up sick again.

Knowing that my business would suffer closure after closure, in January 2021, I started training as a driving instructor. It was an instinctive decision and I'd learned to trust my instincts and went with it. I figured that I needed something people were desperate to get back to – not an industry they only came back to once the rest of their life was sorted.

As it turned out, being a driving instructor ended up being the only industry in which I – the unvaccinated – could continue to work. Not everything has a completely silver lining though because, sadly, it was also the industry that led to the health issues I later developed.

I'd just spent years getting my life healthy and moving, and I was determined this wouldn't be forever, and that I wouldn't go back to sitting down all day again. Yet, despite only seeing it as a secondary, but necessary, form of employment that I wouldn't ever be doing in a full-time capacity, I eventually had no choice.

Mandates

When the vaccine mandates finally came in November 2021, I found I wasn't going to be allowed to reopen my studio. Quite simply, being unvaccinated meant that I couldn't personally work in my own business, and nor could I allow members to enter if they weren't vaccinated. It was then I had to make the hard decision to shut my business down at a time that signalled the end of lockdown for everyone else. There was no other viable option, and I told myself it was the logical thing to do – over a span of two years, my business had been closed for the equivalent of one full year. It wasn't going to work and, once again, I did as I was told.

By this stage, I'd been working for seven months in my new – temporary – job. I'd been quite happy with my two-and-a-half days a week commitment but, overnight, courtesy of a very fortunate set of rules and regulations around this particular industry that saw vaccination only being highly advised rather than compulsory, it became the only job I was allowed to do with my unvaccinated status. For me, this meant I never once worked illegally as an unvaccinated driving instructor.

Being my only available source of income, I found myself working 10 to 12 hours a day, four days a week. The demand was massive, especially for my area and particularly because I had a rare manual specialty.

As a person with a pre-existing medical condition – and having already survived brain surgery once – once those mandates came in I was told that if I had concerns about being vaccinated, I should speak to my doctor. Again, I did as I was told, despite the fact I believed the choice should have been mine. How I felt about vaccination should have been enough. As a person who had taken extreme measures for my health, in terms of my work life, stress management, and careful control of what I put in my body, vaccination wasn't an easy ask for me.

Since my brain surgery, I'd looked at life a lot differently and promised myself I would never again push away my body's warning signs that things weren't right. After being heavily medicated for two years prior to my surgery and suffering all the effects, I can now say that, in nearly thirteen years, I have probably taken six medications in total. I am talking about everything here, from getting rid of birth control to not taking headache or period pain tablets. I was discharged from hospital three days after my brain surgery with a bag full of medication and refused to take any of it. Instead, I rested – completely – for three weeks and slept the pain away, slowly rehabbing my body. Although, rather stupidly, I returned to work too soon. I also stopped adding unnecessary chemicals by way of makeup and hairspray – I was never big for them anyway, so that part was fairly easy. And for years, I wouldn't even take supplements.

And I did go to my doctor. My secondary doctor anyway – the one I occasionally went to when I couldn't get into my regular one. Visiting your doctor about your concerns was sold as a decision that would be easy to make. It should have been easy. It wasn't.

"You can't have Astra Zeneca," the doctor told me. "Novavax may be a better option for a person with your history …" A few taps on the keyboard. Novavax wasn't available in Australia. "but I'm not allowed to write you an exemption to wait for it." She looked straight at me. I knew what was coming. "So we have to discuss Pfizer." A pause. "I believe it will be safe for you but I'm happy to refer you back to your neurologist to ask that question. She can address your concerns as she's more aware of your neurological history."

My initial concerns had only been heightened by a GP who left me feeling she didn't want to give the final okay without support from an expert. But, the thing was, that I was more than happy for her to be like that and was thankful she wasn't a pushy GP, doing what she were told – just get everyone across the line.

Unfortunately, there was going to be a long wait for an appointment to get that expert opinion – as there is for any specialist worth their weight in gold – and moreover, my neurologist worked inside a hospital. Normally, hospital-based appointments were not an issue but, owing to those mandates, I wasn't allowed anywhere near a hospital, let alone inside one.

"You can use telehealth," I was told.

Sure, I certainly could have had my neurologist appointment this way, but if you've ever been unfortunate enough to need a neurologist appointment, you would also know they do a series of tests on you when you visit to check your cognitive function. I was not going to pay $500 to have my neurologist tell me her thoughts about my cognitive function, based on what she saw through a screen. Total waste of money!

With my useless referral in hand, I was left to make my decision alone – to not get vaccinated and thereby become a member of society who was barely able to exist within it. I had to just believe in myself that I had made the right choice. And without the medical backing, it became a choice that a lot of people not only didn't agree with, but a choice that somehow gave people the right to make their own judgements about 'the type of person' I was without ever asking me why I made my decision.

Unpopular decision

We live in a society where we believe we have the right to know things instead of asking respectful questions in an open and curious way. In recent years, as an 'inclusive' society, we have touted 'HERstory', 'use your voice' and other token gestures aimed at campaigning for a right to be heard.

Yet, few asked why I decided not to vaccinate. It wasn't their business apparently. However it was their business to ask if I was vaccinated. It was their business to ask if I knew how stupid I was being. It was their business to try to change my mind. But it was never their business to ask why. No-one was ever supposed to attempt to understand an anti-vaxxer.

Of those who did ask, some did so without any form of judgement and no need to turn my words around and convince me I was wrong. Others didn't. Many didn't make it past the word 'unvaccinated' and some even decided I was no longer worthy of basic respect and therefore had no right to take up human space. At the very least, they were scared to be near me.

The vitriolic people, on the other hand, were not afraid of me. When people are afraid, they do everything they can to get away from you. To the contrary, they wanted to get up in my face. They wanted to get closer and point directly at it. Their first reaction wasn't to be safe; their reaction was to prove they were right. They moved closer to me, while telling me I was a ticking time bomb.

The hypocrisy blew me away. The very same people who were telling me I was 'damaging their health' were also the people who refused to give up smoking or drinking, or didn't deal with past traumas. They were people who were working or eating themselves to death, or never moving their bodies.

They didn't fear me, they feared having to admit they were responsible for the current state of their own health. They feared this respiratory virus would easily upset the unhealthy host they were responsible for maintaining. It was easier to blame me at the last step than work on the foundations of where the problem started.

So when given a free pass for their excuses they went with it. Parroting the science broadcast to us without actually understanding it?

Not a single person who went on an accusatory rant attempted to show any real-life experience dealing with Covid; they just repeated government rhetoric, and the hatred and disgust they were told to have.

If they had sat down and told me they were scared and that an opinion like mine was jarring to them, I would've respected that and encouraged a conversation. If they'd shared with me that they were immune-compromised and were concerned about being in my space, I would have respected that and encouraged a conversation. If they'd shared that they had friends and family members who'd died or suffered from Covid, I would've respected that and encouraged a conversation.

No-one said these things.

Fear was rarely displayed, just disgust for my choices and an attitude that I should've known better. Even the fear wasn't an instinctive, genuine fear; it was a manufactured one from the government and carried by a media agenda – a little something I'd had twenty or so years of experience with. Selling a story. Presenting the most sensational angle. A version of the truth. Always one-sided. Masquerading as well-researched from all angles but often overlooking the genuine reality.

The one thing that got me through the first eighteen months of the pandemic was the ability to discuss with friends, or my trusty journal, what I was feeling. It was the ability to set goals regarding how I was going to help myself and be truly responsible for my physical and mental health. For eighteen months, it worked. This could be largely attributed to the collective feeling in Melbourne and the fact there were so many people around me, going through the same thing, that such conversations became normal. The importance of talking was the new trend and I loved it.

The more I used my own tools, the better I was. I could survive having to close my business. I could survive having to stay at home on my own for twenty-three hours a day. I could survive needing to sell my house. I could survive the constant bombardment of case numbers and deaths, and still be realistic about it while teaching my clients and supporting my friends to do the same.

Reopening

In November 2021, all that changed.

The ability to speak my truth out loud diminished. I became an instant outsider in the eyes of the media and the government. Any suggestion to the contrary was incredibly hurtful, especially when it came through the online taunts of friends and former colleagues, many who actually knew my situation but still chose to speak out about 'people like Lauren'. I knew I had the power to change how I felt, but the tools I used were suddenly no longer available to me. I needed to be able to say what I felt and what I needed, yet I was labelled as a person who didn't have the right to speak.

I couldn't express who I was.

Every conversation ended up being one I had to walk away from before anyone asked me. I gave really vague reasons for not attending events. I had to suggest open spaces for catch-ups without letting on why. I had to make an inventory, 'categorising' friendships according to who was most concerned about Covid and the anti-vaxxers, who was just doing what they were told but really didn't have an opinion, who actually sympathised with this bullshit two-tiered situation – and those who believed the earth was flat.

Then, I had to spread my time accordingly so I could savour my energy and not be burdened with it. I tried as hard as I could to still be the same person, but it meant having four different levels regarding the depth to which I was willing to communicate. Many friendships suffered because of that. I even made the decision, for a friend, to go to two events I wasn't supposed to attend; they were too important for me to miss and I also didn't want to have the conversation as to why, with months of notice, I suddenly couldn't attend. I spent most of the time stressed about being caught out. In making the decision to attend those two events, I had to learn new skills when it came to evading the 'Covid passport' question. I had to have a whole arrival process that didn't involve anyone else being with me unless they were distracted. I felt like I did in the early 2000s when I was baking an alcohol bottle into a loaf of bread and spending hours slowly removing the top of a water bottle trying not to break the seal so I didn't have to spend every cent I'd earned to drink at a music festival. This time though, I was effectively smuggling myself – this illegal contraband – firstly into my friend's hen night and then into her wedding.

I broke the rules once again for the Boxing Day premiere of *The Matrix Reloaded*. It was basically calling me to attend and seemed the perfect event in which to say, 'Fuck the system!'

These might seem like simple things to you, and you may wonder if anyone ever cared that much – but if you were an unvaccinated person in those moments, you'll know they cared. They cared a lot. In fact, they cared so much they didn't care if they belittled you in front of friends and strangers. They totally believed you deserved everything you had coming to you – and worse. If you jump on social media from around that time, people like me were not only the laughing stock, but the new group that deserved to be horrendously trolled. I had people telling me I deserved to die and trying to make me feel as if society would never hold a place for me again.

To this very day – as I am writing this – there are people on donor lists, waiting for major life-saving surgery, who are being denied because they are not vaccinated for Covid.

This has not gone away. And it is incredibly inhumane.

For me, the energy it took to research what the processes of each venues were, was physically and emotionally draining. Would it be easy to get through the entrance or were they going to be strict? Would I be able to arrive on my own without being seen; just in case I had to suddenly turn around and lie about being sick when I didn't get in? All of this was too stressful because I knew how harsh the backlash would be when people found out. I didn't have the energy to make a scene about how unfair the system was. I really had nothing left. I didn't want to rock the boat. I didn't want to have a struggling small business punished for my attendance. I wanted people to not care how I chose to live my life and just let me live it. Being treated like an outsider, I became so small and struggled to find my voice. The last thing I could handle was the excess barrage that unfurled when someone learned my truth.

In the pre-Covid world, things like this never fazed me because the haters would be few and far between and I had my rock-solid crew. But now, my crew was as small as it could possibly be, and the haters were everywhere. The situation had been reversed and everyone felt like they needed to state their opinion on the issue. Even some of 'my crew' were struggling and didn't know what to do or what to say.

Eventually, I no longer had it in me to have a hard conversation every second of every day. I stopped wanting to communicate with people – being beaten down so much can do that to a person. I became the most insular I've ever been in my life. All good self-help books talk about the importance of community when it comes to continuing to enjoy your life – but I felt I had the smallest possible community there was.

Everyone was desperate to get back out and about and, as events went ahead, I became a problem that was too hard to deal with. Should I be invited? Should they feel guilty because they wanted to go somewhere I couldn't go? Why should they have to change their lives to accommodate me when they'd just spent the last two years not living their lives to accommodate the entire state?

I stopped wanting to socialise in any form. The longer I stayed away, the harder it became to go out – even after mandates were lifted. Even now.

Somehow, I'd become someone who was trying to hide who they really were. I hadn't been that way for a long time and it affected my ability to coach my clients. How could I teach them to have a voice when I wasn't using mine?

I'd had to state I'd closed my business for financial reasons, even though I hadn't.

I had to bide my time, saying I was looking at other options before deciding whether to go back to teaching Pilates and yoga, even though I wasn't.

I had to make it look like I was really into having my dinner at home and not attending the local restaurants.

There was an assumption that, because I wasn't vaccinated, I was also breaking all the rules. I wasn't. However, while I was waiting for the mandate to end, I did find ways to do things that did fit within the rules. I taught at a retreat. I ran my own retreat. By that stage, accommodation wasn't a problem, but I couldn't tell anyone else in case they cared. I also regularly submitted to Covid testing – it was one of the rules for my driving job. Every time I stepped foot into the

VicRoads offices, I had to provide either a polymerase chain reaction (PCR) result or a RAT. It was a weekly requirement to keep my job, and sometimes up to three times a week. Never once did I register a positive and I have a drawer full of results to prove it. Yet, there are still a few VicRoads testing officers who turn their noses up at me when I walk through the door.

What did I learn throughout this process?

I learned that I did more harm to myself, physically and emotionally, by not owning my truth. Being honest with yourself is the most important thing you can do in life. Listening to your intuition is key and no-one can tell you how to live your life because only you know how.

To be fair, I had a stronger reason for following my own path than many others. I'd had life-altering news before. I'd already done my bit to increase the quality of my life and I couldn't risk it for something that was not tested – it was as simple as that.

I've been asked how I held on throughout it all. The answer is straightforward – I had no choice; I knew what a worse quality of life felt, looked and sounded like.

2022 letter from neurologist

Having made my own decision without backup, for ten months I constantly debated whether I'd made the 'right' decision – even though my body was telling me I had.

It was now September 2022. The time for my neurologist appointment had finally arrived.

> *Lauren previously suffered from a neurological condition in 2009 and she was under my care at the time. As a consequence of this neurological condition, Lauren chose not be vaccinated when the Covid pandemic occurred in 2020. This is her human right and this right should be respected ...*

> ... *This letter is to confirm that I, as her treating neurologist, have advised Lauren that she is **not obliged to be vaccinated for Covid** ...*
>
> *... Vaccination may aggravate or trigger a variety of underlying neurological conditions. It is unknown if her particular underlying neurological condition will be triggered or not. This is the choice that she has made. It is a very reasonable choice, and her personal choice should be respected.*
>
> *Yours Sincerely*
> *Dr Hilary Ann Hunt*
> *Neurologist*
> *20th September 2022*

In that moment, seeing that letter, I felt listened to. I felt truly heard for the first time in two-and-a-half years. I found myself saying 'thank you' sixteen times a minute. I kept feeling the need to justify my responses to her questions before realising she was smiling at me because I didn't need to.

It was hard not to cry. My brain kept questioning whether it had actually happened. I was elated but it also felt weird. This wasn't a flaky, uneducated friend. It wasn't a crazy conspiracy theorist. The person who confirmed that I was right in my belief that I shouldn't get vaccinated was a highly educated medical professional with years of experience in the field of neuroscience – and she was sitting across from me saying, "Vaccination may aggravate a variety of neurological conditions". In front of me was an actual medical professional telling me she supported freedom of choice and, what's more, stated that at no time along this journey should I ever have been told by another medical professional that I should be vaccinated for Covid.

She believed the decision should be mine but, as my neurologist, she would strongly advise me to weigh up the pros and cons of having the vaccination versus not having it. Had I presented for advice this time last year, she would have advised me of the potential for a recurrence of my original condition plus any complications that could arise from getting Covid.

She agreed with all of my arguments – the steps I'd taken to look after my health and minimise a recurrence, the things I'd been doing during the pandemic to raise my immunity, and that, as a driving instructor, it was safer – for me and my students – that I not flare up a previous neurological condition.

"So, what's next?" she asked, like I had the power to take over an army – and for the briefest of moments, I felt like I did.

I wish that elation lasted.

I wish that the strength I'd felt in my own conviction could've seen me return to my old life – where I'd had courage, where I'd been comfortable with who I was, and where I'd felt valued.

But that power – that elation – was short-lived. No-one else cared. Those who'd always supported me treated me no differently. Those who'd stepped away from me were no longer around to hear my justification. Those who'd tiptoed around the situation, trying not to let it end our friendship, very quickly washed over it and didn't want to spent too long speaking about it. People were either shocked that I'd been correct, or were quick to remind me that I was just an isolated case, and that my situation was different but the majority of people still needed to do the right thing.

The damage had already been done to my soul and I didn't have it in me to change a world full of opinions. So, after that initial flurry of excitement, I mostly kept it to myself.

Those who supported me all along were amazing and I thank them for being in my corner every moment of the last few years. The thing was, I wasn't in my corner. I happily stood up for others but felt ashamed to do it for myself.

Still no exemption

With that letter from my neurologist, and her support, you'd think I would've been able to get an exemption.

Quite the opposite.

The letter was written because my neurologist was unable to provide an exemption under the strict rules enforced by the government. At the end of the day, despite her letter, her support and the justification of my choice, I was still a shunned member of society. There were still jobs I couldn't do, places I couldn't travel, and high-risk settings I wasn't allowed to enter – like the nursing home where my Godmother resided.

I had mistakenly thought that obtaining the support of a medical professional to not be vaccinated, particularly when there was significant potential for previous medical conditions to arise, would be enough to gain an exemption.

That was not reality.

I needed to stop telling myself that story – and so did everyone else.

But – what was the reality?

Facing the reality

> *... I support her despite not being able to exempt her ...*

There were two medical conditions – neither of which were mine – that were exempt from vaccination. To get the exemption, your doctor had to prove you had one of those conditions.

Despite my neurologist stating that my condition could also have side effects, the only two conditions that were considered were the ones they definitely knew, without a shadow of doubt, would cause complications – not the ones that 'could'.

FACT – an absolute known side effect of vaccines is that they can create an inflammatory reaction within the body and affect pre-existing inflammatory diseases – in this case, neurological inflammation.

Having already had a neurological condition, I have a higher risk of that inflammation causing a neurological response. The problem with the exemption is that it was limited to conditions that are caused by inflammation only. My condition is caused by physical presentations as well as inflammation – thus not entitled to exemption.

This was a decision made by the government – not by neurologists.

It was a grey area. A technicality. Semantics – the use of the word 'only'. And it saw me outcast by society.

I was an outcast – from a government sense, a checking-into-social-settings sense, a workplace-rules sense, a need-to-shut-down-your-business sense.

That was the reality.

Not vaccinated. Not eligible for exemption. Not allowed to participate. Not allowed to live your life.

Hospitalisation

While I had a letter to show every time I was asked to present my vaccination status, I didn't show anyone at first, other than my closest friends and family. I didn't use it to return to society. I didn't publicly display it on my social media. I didn't use it when I was chastised at VicRoads for actually following their rules by producing a negative Covid test result.

Two months later, in November 2022, I had to use it.

My driving days had become long and my plans to continue doing online movement classes disappeared when most people rejoined society and stopped working out online, at home. I still organised a retreat but my plans to run several were pushed back once the extra effort required to cater for people who weren't vaccinated became apparent and overwhelming. All of this meant I was failing to move my body to the extent I needed.

I ended up with weekly physio and having to see a myotherapist every fortnight for months. Finally, with a majority of the restrictions pertaining to me being dropped, and in the middle of making plans to return to my normal life, the sciatic nerve pain kicked in. I dealt with it for four days, but on that fifth day, the pain was so bad I couldn't get out of bed. I couldn't sit up. I couldn't walk. I was in complete agony.

I was so annoyed with myself.

My body had decided it didn't want to hold out for the final six weeks of work I'd planned before a long break at the end of the year and took me on an unexpected trip to the emergency department of a Melbourne hospital.

Despite screaming in agony as I tried to walk through the front doors of the hospital, I suddenly had to prove I was worthy of care. "Can we see your vaccination status," I was asked, ever so politely.

I'd had the presence of mind to ring my neurologist's office on the way to emergency and they told me to make sure I had the letter with me. This is what I handed over as I was in the foyer, being held upright while someone went to get a trolley. Three nurses passed it to each other, reading it and trying to decide what to do.

In the interim, I'd been masked up and shoved on a hospital trolley while being asked questions about my visit. Each new person who turned up was first told I was an unvaccinated patient.

The obvious agony I was in appeared to be secondary to the more pressing question regarding exactly how I'd obtained this letter. Yes – I was asked exactly that.

That lit a fire under me, and the voice of my neurologist asking, "So what's next?" reminded me I had a duty to do something. I didn't want to keep being a second-rate citizen, the person who everyone's lockdown aggression is pinned on. And I certainly didn't want to be made to feel like I was responsible for Covid deaths in Melbourne when a hospital was showing me they cared more about my vaccination status than my welfare.

Eventually, I was admitted. Perhaps they rang her to make sure it was legit.

The diagnosis was degeneration between L4 and L5, L5 and S1. This had pushed my disc out sideways, causing it to come into contact with the sciatic nerve and giving me four nights in hospital with the added bonus of being told spinal surgery was my only option.

It annoyed me that my body was calling the shots.

'I had plans,' I told it. 'Surely you could have waited another six weeks.' I was planning on recuperating then.

'No,' my body replied. 'I'm sick of you waiting to see if everything is fine. I don't want to hide anymore. I don't want to be mistreated anymore.'

Fuck! It was a fine time for my body to let me know who was boss.

It was a sad irony. The industry that saved me from joining the ranks of the unemployed became the one that caused excruciating nerve pain to return to my body. I'd changed my entire life to not end up in hospital on morphine for nerve pain – and then ended up that way thanks to the one industry the government allowed me to work in.

After refusing surgery, leaving the hospital, rehabbing myself and seeing a myotherapist for nerve flossing, something in my early recovery process for the sciatica set off the trigeminal nerve on the opposite side of my face just a few weeks later.

I went to the dentist, hoping to rule it out. I knew what the pain was – I'd been here before – but I wanted to be told I was wrong.

In the brief moments of relief I had between my screams, tears and inability to actually open my mouth for an assessment, the dentist confirmed my fears. Again, this was not a bad toothache but appeared to be pain associated with an inflamed trigeminal nerve. This time on my good side. Luckily the majority of the facial pain dissipated by the fourth day but then began the long process of recovery for the sciatic nerve and its associated back, leg and foot pain, without aggravating or trapping any other nerves in my body. So far it has worked. It has been a slow and measured process to incorporate a whole reset of my nervous system – working with my myotherapist, taking some medication for a short period of time, dealing with lost sleep and limited function without succumbing to the stress and mental anguish of rehabilitation. It took a year to get back to the point where I was almost myself again. A year of frustration, fighting fear and learning to trust the process again. Ultimately, a healthy reminder of why I make these choices for myself.

Despite my original physical presentation of TN all those years ago, what I managed to prove was that my condition can actually be set off by inflammation. It was a small win in the realm of 'being right' but the shittiest of ways to find out. I never really wanted to know the answer to that question but, in the end, I didn't even need a vaccination to find out.

Thailand

We all have a place we go to heal and for me it's Thailand and I was dying to get there and start to repair.

Over the years, Thailand has completely changed me as a person. At the end of the Covid lockdowns and mandates, one thing I knew for certain was that I wanted a trip back to my beloved second home.

It was already booked – two months after my hospital stay. The doctor told me I wouldn't be leaving the hospital without spinal surgery. He said I'd never train in Muay Thai again. He said I definitely wouldn't be getting on that plane to Thailand in January.

But I knew better.

My body craves the comfort of that place and as crazy as my doctor thought I was when I signed all the forms to say I was refusing treatment and checked myself out of the hospital, I knew that if I was going to heal, Thailand was the only place I would.

Since 2014 I've visited around nine times. It's a place where everything seems to come together and each time I've been there, it has had a profound impact on me. Often, I've returned home after making some of the biggest decisions of my life.

My first life-changing experience was at a retreat called Phuket Cleanse in Rawai, a southern province of Phuket. I went for the fitness, scoffed at the wellness workshops because "I don't need that soppy shit; I'm not depressed", and left realising it was the one thing I'd been missing all along.

I was a black-and-white thinker up until this point. I was on the general treadmill of thinking that if I just attained certain things in life, and kept ticking them off – house, tick; car, tick; career, tick; finances, tick; husband, still working on it; children, still working on it; perfect body, that's why I'm here – then I'd done it right. Each thing was getting me closer to this elusive thing they call happiness.

I went, thinking I'd ticked off four of the seven goals, and the reason why I felt like I wasn't completely happy was because I still had three more life goals to complete. The sad thing is that most of us are wired this way, and we also not only believe that our happiness is linked to successful completion of these big tick items, but that each item is intrinsically linked to the next. To achieve happiness, you have to be great at juggling, or at least making progress in all seven areas at once.

I went there with my first four ticked off, thinking that the perfect physique would get me a husband, which would eventually get me the children. And then what? I've cracked the game of life? No more levels? Complete domination of my happiness?

Did I really believe that the end goal was to no longer have any goals?

Tick! Now I just live in this exact frozen feeling of time for the rest of my life.

I was thirty-two at the time. Did I expect that happiness would come from never having to try? That I wouldn't need to do anything ever again to feel happy and content? What a boring life that would be. And if there is one thing I struggle with in life, it's the boring and mundane.

I am almost embarrassed to say that I thought this just nine years ago. However, if I look back at my life up until that time, it is a totally reasonable thought to have considering the way I lived, the life I'd been exposed to and the little time I'd had for reflection. I was my own example of how each person's story affects how they see life.

When I was younger, I remember not being able to go anywhere on my own. I'd always gone places with family, but when I had friends who wanted to meet me somewhere, it was the scariest thing in the world. What if I rock up alone – will people think I'm lonely and have no friends? What if I walk into a venue the wrong way and, God forbid, have to stop and turn around … in front of everyone? These are the things that made it hard for me to do things on my own back in the day. But I did.

I was the youngest of my siblings, by a long way, and never had someone my age to do stuff with in the house. I had to be independent and it scared the hell out of me. The more I did it, the more I could tell myself it was going to be fine. No-one is watching, no-one is laughing, no-one is paying any attention to what you are doing.

Just do you and don't look up.

Then it became easier. It was the same as the first time I travelled on my own – what if I get lost, or worse? What if? What if? What if? It was always the same. I had to learn to ignore the what-ifs, breathe deeply and work things out along the way. Everything was going to be okay.

Thailand was a place that made me see that my stresses in life wouldn't exist outside of my own mind – if I could just take the time to sit and observe. It was a place that made me think 'what if I've been viewing my place in this world all wrong?' It became a place that gave space and perspective, and that helped me make big decisions about life. And I went back, again and again, and made more. I eventually left my career after decisions made in Thailand. The country saw me leave Australia three times to work for extended periods overseas. I started the basis of my business in Thailand. I even wrote most of this book in Thailand.

The universe works in funny ways. It asks you how much you really want something. My trip to Thailand in January 2023 was going to be about rehab, a little Muay Thai and finishing and publishing this book – and I nearly didn't get into the country.

It was fitting that the debacle was all about Thailand temporarily reinstating their vaccination passport on 9 Jan 2023.[17] This happened to be six days before I was due to fly into the country, so I panic-bought a same-day flight, which got me there one hour before cut-off. They enforced it hard for a whole twenty-four hours – and then dropped it the following day in the midst of a major outcry from all over the world.

I woke up on a regular Sunday morning knowing I had one more week left in Melbourne before my glorious four-week holiday in Thailand. I was even going to brunch that day. As I was scrolling randomly through Instagram at 9:45 am, I saw a post about new entry requirements into Thailand – starting from the 9th! What? That was tomorrow. If the entry requirements included vaccination status, I wouldn't be going on my holiday!

And there it was – unvaccinated people were not going to be allowed in from 9 January.

Today was the 8th.

I was booked on a flight on the 14th.

I was not missing this!

Springing into action, I tried to change my flight but it was no use because the next flight went via Singapore and still didn't get me in until the morning of the 9th. I tried Jetstar, a company that had stopped some of my friends from flying internationally during this whole mess, and when I initially booked my flights, I wasn't allowed to board their planes.

A quick read of the rules and regulations stated that Jetstar had recently dropped their international flight mandate. There was a 3 pm flight that very day. This meant I had to be at the airport by 12 pm.

I better hurry the fuck up!

Never before had I booked a same-day flight. I'd never had a mere two hours to pack, book an Uber, clean my house up for the family staying when I was away, book accommodation, organise travel insurance and actually get all the way to the airport from my house – which was a 45-minute drive in good traffic! Never. Until this day. My saving grace was that, by chance, I'd picked up my international currency from the bank on Friday and I'd also done a little search the day before and pulled together items for international travel – passport, power points, padlocks, all the little gadgets – and put them all in one drawer. I grabbed it all, shoved it in a suitcase and then filled it with clothes. Yet, I couldn't believe that I made it.

But it was only the first step.

I was concerned I'd get asked for a whole bunch of documentation when I got to the counter because I'd printed nothing. It was the most stressed I'd been in years. That was my first real win – despite a policy that was about to be implemented, in a matter of hours, the Jetstar counter was particularly lax. I checked myself in. I handled my own baggage. I had a one-way ticket and didn't need to prove I was coming back, or that I had any Covid-related travel insurance, or even if I was indeed the person on the passport and listed in the booking. I didn't need to show anyone anything – except my boarding pass. No need to show my passport and I hadn't even put my passport number on the form when I booked online that morning. Immigration is self-serve – either very relaxed or too hard to fake.

No-one asked me a thing. And I didn't have to speak to anyone to enter another country.

Then we sat on the tarmac for two-and-a-half hours. All I could think about was the time.

First there were no staff to load water on to the plane. Then no staff to load baggage onto the plane. Then there was an engineering fault – which is something you never want to hear. (Seriously, if you're a pilot, just make it up – say it's still the water.)

At one point, the guy sitting next to me said, "Hurry up and get this bird in the air; I'm not vaccinated." I had to laugh. Same, buddy! Same.

So, my last-minute flight that was meant to land just after 8 pm, finally arrived around 10:30 pm. And then began the nervous wait to see if we'd get off and through customs before 12 am. Once we were in the airport, I checked my phone.

In the eight hours I'd been in the air, the rules had changed four times!

The first change added the requirement of a note from your doctor. Technically, I had this, although I doubt Jetstar would have let me on without an actual exemption. The second change was that if you couldn't provide documents on arrival, you would need to do a test at the Thai airport. The third required the possession of Covid travel insurance if you weren't vaccinated, didn't have a letter or had to be tested on arrival. The final change, which had come through during our last hour in the air, was the announcement of more massive changes in the next few hours.

I was through customs by 11:15 pm. After all the stress, the rush and the waiting, it was actually the easiest entry into a country I believe I've ever had. The next day, however, was a different story for some people.

On Monday, one of our retreat teachers boarded her flight in Sydney and was asked for all of her documentation – the difference of a day! However, by the time she was in the air, that fourth change came through officially: due to massive backlash worldwide, the new introductory measures were scrapped, a mere ten hours after being implemented.

Yes, it cost me an extra $1200 for a one-way flight, $300 for extra accommodation, $50 or so for longer insurance – not to mention the loss of money for a flight I didn't take and the fastest beating heart I've had in a long time – but the peace of mind was worth it. I would not have wanted to stay in Melbourne for that whole week wondering whether they were going to change the rules or what would happen if they cancelled people's entries again.

But it was okay. I'd made it. I was in possession of four pairs of pants, three pairs of shorts, eight tops and a random collection of underwear. Sure, I'd forgotten some vital pieces for a sunshine beach Muay Thai holiday – I had no sunscreen or boxing gloves – but nothing that couldn't be purchased. Although, anyone who has visited Thailand knows that the two most expensive things you can buy there are gloves and sunscreen. Nothing is ever as bad as you first think. There is always a way.

I saw it as the universe testing me to see how badly I wanted this trip. It was my first in nearly four years. I wanted to forget the year that was 2022 and start being myself again. Start making my own decisions. Start standing up for myself and being free to be who I was. I could have thrown in the towel and given up – that might have been cheaper

– but I wanted to be there and I got there in the end. And I used that extra six days to write about my life in the last few years, and release the trauma of it all.

After everything ...

How many others do you know who have a story similar to mine?

Who do you know who had an extremely valid reason for not being vaccinated, or even a reason for waiting for further evidence of its effectiveness before making their decision?

Who do you know who was relegated to wearing the title of 'dirty anti-vaxxer' or 'crazy conspiracy theorist' for their hesitance?

Now, with scientific backup that vaccination is 'just good protection against Covid', how many of those people do you believe were right to take their chances and not worry about getting vaccinated at all because it is their human right to make that decision?

Being completely honest, this whole experience has now made me the most anti-vaccination I've ever been in my life. Three years on and I'm almost happy to wear that title with pride.

If only it had all been easy to relate to, rather than scary or shunned.

If only we had spent time discussing, communicating and listening, maybe there would have been a solution that everyone was comfortable with. Instead, we pushed people so far they started to find their strength in the extremes.

Your turn

How do you feel now, knowing my story? Has it made you rethink your responses to others whose situations you didn't know? Can you see the importance of arming yourself with information before making decisions? Can you appreciate that others possibly also should have been made exempt and it was not the process you thought?

The Four Per Cent

My Melbourne – then and now

As a city, prior to lockdown, Melbourne got a lot of things right.

I often would comment to my Sydney-sider friends that Melbourne was more inclusive. It had a friendlier vibe. I didn't have to go to one particular area of the city to experience different things I liked. I didn't have to move to a Bondi to live the life of a bronzed beach influencer. I didn't have to trek out to a Byron Bay for spiritual enlightenment. I didn't need to walk the streets of Newtown to share my eclectic self with like-minded individuals. I didn't have to move to a different location to experience live music rather than the same crowd of drunks singing to cover songs. I could get a bit of all of this within ten kilometres of my home, and each destination would contain a mix of open and supportive people. There was a choice of great cultural restaurants, large parks, garden areas and beaches where I could hang with like-minded friends, and enjoy fitness activities and other random hobbies while discovering new and interesting things to do – all in the one area.

These days, however, if you were to look up 'division' in a dictionary, it wouldn't be wrong to see Melbourne as one of the word's definitions.

You are woke or you're not.

You are good or bad.

You are worthy or scum.

If you didn't get vaccinated, you couldn't possibly be anything other than a consumer of Murdoch media, a One Nation supporter, a racist, a homophobe and a No-voter in The Voice referendum.

Asking questions is now a failure to comply.

Wanting body autonomy labels you as a ticking time bomb.

Prioritising your health makes you dangerous.

None of these things are true but they all make you less likely to be an ignorant consumer. And that is dangerous – just not to yourself.

Issues in society are no longer talked about. Everything is a hard yes or hard no; there is no middle ground.

Life doesn't operate like that – it never has – so why do the residents of Melbourne suddenly believe it does? Have we all decided we are no longer on a quest to become the best version of ourselves? Do we no longer want to keep learning? Do we not want to ask questions? Do we want to avoid robust discussion?

Do we not want to get a full understanding of our place in this world?

In Melbourne, we have all stopped in time and given in to what we are told to do. Given in to the most popular opinion. We're having the soft conversations. We're being seen to be doing the right thing. We're giving up because we can't be bothered.

I am guilty of this right now, so there's no judgement.

We haven't healed from the last few years. We're living like 'life' is going to be taken away from us again, so what's the use in trying? We're non-committal. We don't make plans. We have no goals. We're all just getting by.

I suspect most people don't understand where these feelings come from and have just accepted it's the way we are now. Very few realise it's because we haven't addressed this point in time, taken a look back at where we were, compared it to what we then become and decided how we want to move forward.

I did my own stocktake of this theory when I decided to pack up all my belongings and leave this town. My decision to move out of Melbourne by the end of 2023 had me sorting through the belongings I need to box up, need to sell and need to just give away.

What a time to do a trip down memory lane! Sure, let's look through the relics of my life while I'm feeling despondent and like my life hasn't amounted to what I thought it would be by now. Let's sift through my memories when I feel stuck, like there's no point in attempting to move forward.

Each important thing that hadn't made it out of a box from the last time I moved reminded me of how far I had come.

There were academic certificates: a Bachelor's degree, a two-year diploma and two different Certificate IVs for two very different industries.

There were piles of study notes in the areas of media, television broadcasting, road safety and driver training, Pilates, yoga, boxing, Muay Thai, Reiki, mindfulness, meditation and mindset coaching.

There were business flyers from when I owned an aerial yoga and Pilates studio.

Hours of footage of documentaries I produced and edited, both here and overseas.

Drafts of the renovation I designed for my unit. Sales contracts of the two homes I owned and later sold.

PDFs of workshops I ran in exotic locations abroad and for companies in Melbourne who were trying to help their staff through lockdown.

I found thirty-something staples from my brain surgery, still in the specimen container and the paperwork from my most recent hospital stay that I had to sign to say I was refusing their invasive spinal treatment.

All of this made me do a 'stop and check' on where I've been and where I'm at after forty-one years. I know a lot about myself. I know a lot about the world I live in. I know a lot about where I feel safe and comfortable in my own skin.

Melbourne is no longer my place.

My home for the last twenty-one years now makes me feel like an alien who merely inhabits it.

When I walk the streets, it doesn't feel the same. The inner city is lifeless. Shops are closed. Few people smile. Diners at the sidewalk cafes are talking about others, or how much they hate their own lives. Everyone has aged about ten years. To get things done, I have to deal with people who don't have the energy to take pride in their work anymore. Businesses are understaffed. Body language gives many away before they falsely respond to my "How are you?" with "Good, thanks". It feels like not a single person has any remaining tolerance. Quite a few people start conversations by trying to pick a fight.

It's exhausting.

We are all tired.

There are fleeting moments of community that tide us over – excitement for a sporting team's Premiership match, or a new Netflix show to discuss with our peers. Sadly, though, there's not much beyond that. We don't seem excited for anything other than packing our bags and leaving the city. The problem is, we have reached peak groundhog day – we're all on a hamster wheel we feel powerless to get off.

I am despondent with life.

But mostly, I am despondent with Melbourne.

At some point, I believe we all contemplate the meaning of life in our own way. I don't think any of us actually work out exactly where it starts; we just have an overriding feeling that there is something else out there.

My experiences of the world, along with three years of lockdown that provided many hours alone with my thoughts, prompted me to realise that 'this is my life' and I am living it. Life is about whether I can discover wonder each and every day without being drawn in to the drama that society tries to involve me in. It's about learning about your impact on this world every day and deciding how you want to show up in it, and which parts of it you want to focus on. It's about finding the joy, experiencing the sadness, and feeling a range of emotions in between. Once you can do that, you can go back and spend the majority of your time where your soul is free.

The true journey is seeing how far you are willing to go to find yourself under the illusion of constraint regarding who you believe you are supposed to be.

I feel my journey in Melbourne has ended. It no longer makes me happy. And being happy is the meaning of this life.

How did we get to such divisiveness and judgement of others with the need to point out all our differences?

How have I gotten to a place where I no longer enjoy anything about Melbourne, with its angst and division, and want to get the hell out of here?

Your turn

Go for a walk in your hometown. What do you notice? What has changed? What has stayed the same? Is it still a place you feel you belong? What will you do about it?

The Four Per Cent

Part 3:

The lessons

I witnessed a lot of contradiction in my own circles.

People complaining about others not doing the right thing and then choosing which rules they themselves were happy to follow. Expressing concern for their health if someone stood less than 1.5 metres behind them at the supermarket while they were ringing in their trolley purchases of highly processed food, alcohol and cigarettes. Sharing memes about idiots who didn't wear their masks properly, while being the first people to complain about putting it on when it was hot. Going on random Tinder dates and hooking up with people whose health habits they knew nothing about just so they could leave their own houses, yet expecting the masked strangers walking towards them to cross the road as they passed. Starting conversations about how 'others' aren't taking a major health crisis seriously, but never looking at their own daily behaviours.

We all knew these people. At times, we have all been them. In a global pandemic it's easy to feed off the drama and lose track of your own contribution to it. But a pandemic is not the only time we get caught up in these cycles. It happens when we can't process emotion.

When we can't identify the emotion we are really feeling. When we are feeling down, stressed or tired. When things change and we feel uncomfortable. When we don't feel respected or are triggered by memories of our past.

It happens because we are human.

The first step is recognising it. The toughest part is to challenge yourself to change your response.

Every person will take a different amount of time to gain recognition, and a longer period of time to actively change their behaviours. The first thing I ask all my clients to do is work out where they currently sit on that journey, and then respond to the question: "Does life happen to you or do you create it?" If they believe they create it – does the language they use every day accurately reflect someone who is fully in charge of their life?

You'll have heard many of the following sentences: "I had to do this today,"; "He made me,"; "If they would just stop doing that, life would be better,"; and "Once I get through this, everything will be fine".

We all use these lines.

None of them are true.

I've grown to love it when my friends call me out on them, and am even prouder when, as a crazy woman talking to herself, I recognise them as I say them, and then re-frame my sentence.

"This is important to get done today."

"I've agreed to this but next time I might need to set better boundaries and say no."

"It's not personal. I shouldn't let this affect me."

"I'm upset by this and need to have a conversation with that person about how it has made me feel."

"I'm not really feeling like I have time to myself. I have to prioritise what needs to be done and delegate the rest."

"I need more time to do this thing I enjoy. Life is not feeling great right now and I need to prioritise my mental health."

"I need to ask for help."

Your burden is yours alone to shift, but choose the right people to share it with.

Sadly, as each person realises this in their own time, there will be a change in friendships. Despite loving you unconditionally, some people may back away to give you the chance to do your own work. Unless you're aware, you'll probably feel less supported and decide they are the problem.

No-one else is ever the problem; it's how you handle the situation.

Ultimately, you have to show up for yourself. One of the hardest things in life is to continue to show up, even when you don't want to. No-one is going to come along and take all of the pain away, it's up to you to process it in a healthy way.

Know who you want to be. To achieve that goal, it's important to start by accepting the person you are right now. Be honest with yourself about whether you're in the right head space to do it now. Get outside help to process the traumas you never speak about. Send some forgiveness to those who have hurt you and, more importantly, keep some for yourself.

Understand it's going to be a journey; a path you'll need to take each day of your life. Sometimes it will be easier, sometimes harder. You'll see a lot of improvement along the way and will occasionally feel sorry for yourself when you feel drawn back into a rut. But, it will be more rewarding and worthwhile than where you are now. That beautiful brain of yours will keep you on your toes and, if nothing else, will remind you that you're alive.

The good news is the brain is an ever-changing and complex beast. Neural pathways can be severely damaged due to early childhood trauma but they are not lost forever. They can be changed. Rewired. It all starts with the belief we can change and the courage to seek the help required to do it. Change takes support. It takes strength. There will be lifestyle adjustments. It takes having the right people around you. All of this is needed until you become the person willing to show up for yourself. Until you can comfortably face who you are.

All of us, at some stage, need to face who we are. In this section of the book, we are going to look at the lessons we can learn from the pandemic and, when we're ready, we're going to face who we were during that time. This is how growth happens.

What lies were we telling ourselves?

What trauma did we not want to face?

What do we need to let go of?

What do we need to work on?

Who can we go to for help with any of the above?

What is our reality and what facts can we provide ourselves with to see how closely our story aligns with it?

Your turn

What is your story? What do you tell yourself about who you are? Does life happen to you or do you create it? If you create your life, how do you show up every day and does your language match that?

The Four Per Cent

How did we get here?

Why do we hide our stories? Why don't we talk about them, process them and analyse them?

As Australians it has a lot to do with how we identify. We have always taken pride in being a bunch of carefree people with a 'she'll be right' mentality. At heart, we are not mass protesters; we only protest when it affects our ego. What I mean by that is we suffer a fear of missing out and need to hold and share popular opinions. We'd go to a group rally as a day out with our friends before we did it for the actual meaning of it. We are so ingrained in this 'every man for himself' culture that we pretend we are bringing others up when, in reality, we only bring them up if it benefits us or our street cred.

We do not have the strong patriotism of America. We did not find ourselves on 'either side of the Berlin Wall' like Germany. We have not found ourselves with one foot in the UK and the other in Europe like the Irish. We are not like a lot of countries that have learned from wars on their doorsteps. We don't have a long celebrated history of our strengths. We weren't able to watch in person as those before us fought to protect what we have because it didn't happen in our own backyards. We have always been 'the ally', fighting for something outside of ourselves. Yet we often mimic the actions of other nations without thinking whether or not it's good for our own.

What we do have, however, is a dark history of invasion that we refuse to acknowledge. A long-lasting act that resulted in a focus on who deserves to belong and call Australia home, and who doesn't. We expected others to give up and accept that we'd arrived. That wasn't a fair fight. We shouldn't be proud of that. Our way of dealing with it over all this time is simply the 'suck it up princess' attitude. We have a long history of covering up and failing to talk about the atrocities we've subjected others to.

Shit that literally wouldn't fly in other countries, especially our discussions in the workplace, just happens here. We're laid back. We love a bit of sexualisation or carnal knowledge in our promotions

– Cu in the NT, down under, map of Tassie. We're not serious, except when it comes to hearing the sound of our own voices. We care, and we're angry when it directly affects us, but not before. And the effect has to be bigger than the effect on our ego. We're a country that suffers tall poppy syndrome. We are very egocentric and never want anyone to show off and do better than us.

We have truly displayed what it means to be a progressive Western country with our fast-paced lifestyle, a demand for everything at our fingertips and little respect for the impact we leave behind. We laugh at America with their first amendment – so strongly a part of who they are and so attached to their history – yet we'll do anything to ignore ours. By not appreciating that our First Nations Peoples knew exactly what to do when it came to living, working with and providing for our natural environment, many of those ways have been completely forgotten. What a waste. It should have been part of our history, never lost and held onto with pride.

A podcast on Triple J[18] suggested that Australia is a country that doesn't really have a third space. Our cities are not really centred around a communal location where everyone comes together. We have no place where everyone feels like they belong, nor are proud of our cities enough to want to share that space with everyone. Sports stadiums are probably the closest we get to this.

What we need is an overhaul, something that will bring back a focus on community.

Strangely enough, the lockdown years prior to the vaccination debate actually made most of us realise what we loved about community life. We found people to walk with. We willingly spent time in our local parks, just sitting in the sun and having a picnic. We broke the online workday up with exercise and visiting our local businesses to buy coffee and a sweet treat.

Then, lockdown ended and before long we'd fallen straight back into old habits.

Park 'hangs' need to make a weekly, if not daily, comeback. Yoga and meditation should be practised and taught in schools. Break time in office environments should be a given. No eating at desks. Go out with your walk buddy. Human Resources departments should deal with venting and give advice without judgement. Journaling – with group participation; no need to share if you don't want to but the one person who does will help others realise they all feel the same.

I'd never felt as connected to my local area in Melbourne as I did during that first year of lockdown. We all could see that we were suffering this upheaval to our lives together. We had compassion for one another. We found respite in the simple things that we'd previously taken for granted. It was hard. It hurt. But it was shared.

We need to get that back.

Your turn

Think about the conversations you had with others during the Covid lockdowns. Maybe Covid was our only topic of conversation at the time, but at least we were talking and everyone was asking after each other. Have that conversation now, with this page or, better still, with someone else. How are you? What tasks have you taken up? Have you spoken to anyone else? Have you had a chance to walk outside this week?

The lessons

How we speak matters

The way we currently communicate with one another needs to change. Conversation is key – being able to listen respectfully and answer questions without shutting people and their concerns down is key. Get rid of the belief that you know better. Stop always trying to have the last say. Start a discussion with those who may not see your point of view but don't bully them in to doing what you believe is right. Bullying never made anyone understand.

These days, nothing is clear-cut for me when it is presented as an issue. The more someone wants to scream an opinion at me or thrust a single-sided story down my throat on a daily basis with their Instagram posts, the more I think about the people directly involved. I think about the opinions expressed and how they are presented. I look for the answers in the stories of those people who are trying to tell me how to think and feel, and wonder what got them to this moment in their life. Most importantly, however, I've learned to listen to what is actually being said, without any preconceived ideas or emotions.

I firmly believe that despite this reflection being the hardest thing I've had to learn to do, it has been the number one thing that has changed my mindset and shifted me into the person I most want to be – someone who listens to understand and asks respectful questions to gain clarity. No judgement. No emotion. Just respect and a willingness to learn.

But it's hard when very few other people are conversing with you in that way.

If you want to win an argument, treating people with contempt is not the way to do it. Neither is making generalised assumptions about the way people do or should feel. Nor can you shame someone into making what you think is a good decision. And you certainly can't, on the one hand, say how important it is to support an issue and then, on the other, tell people it doesn't actually affect them when they ask questions about it.

We shouldn't treat each other like this, and neither should our government. This is why they can take responsibility for the result in the 2023 referendum of The Voice to Parliament. That argument was exactly that – an argument shooting down the other side. Labelling them racist. Telling others it doesn't make any difference to their lives so just vote yes. An inability to have a conversation and respectful discussion that was void of contempt was what lost that vote – not a majority of Australians being racist.

After all the Covid lockdowns and forced mandates, is the government so out of touch that it cannot see that it simply does not work to just tell people what to do and label them as conspiracy theorists if they ask questions? Even if they thought it did back then, during the pandemic, surely they've realised it doesn't now. They think they can make changes by saying these won't affect you during the middle of a 'cost of living' crisis, and post a lockdown that destroyed businesses and created high interest rates. Do they think we've forgotten the shit-load of money wasted on two-year-late quarantine facilities, the Commonwealth Games debacle and submarines we won't see for another decade? Was guilting people the only way to get their vote?

We have allowed the recent vaccine division to continue to divide us on everything, and the government is setting the precedent. This is what needs to be addressed. We are heading down a dark path. Crime is on the rise. Anti-Semitism is on the rise. We have lost our compassion, our ability to understand and our ability to see commonality.

We are all humans in this big world – and we've lost sight of that fact.

I feel so bad for First Nations Peoples in this country. The government has used them as a political pawn and contributed to further displaced trauma. I hope in the future you will see this wasn't a racist decision by a majority of people.

I hope this is a lesson to everyone on how to accurately encourage respectful conversation and not have such a hard line view on every issue.

I think in the last few years we have all learned a few lessons.

Lesson 1: Validation

For two-and-a-half years I continued to do what I believed was best for me. I packed up my business under government rules. I lost friends due to judgement. I wasn't allowed in social settings. I couldn't make any money. I needed to sell my home. I was made to feel like a leper, like I was only person in the room who would be responsible if someone died. Two-and-a-half years, I stood by my convictions and then, finally, an actual medical professional told me I'd done the right thing.

What is your first thought when you are finally validated after a long period?

Is it processing how it feels to hear you made the right decision? Is it thinking about how it feels to know that each person who didn't support you – those who always found it in themselves to remind you that you weren't a medical professional or a scientist and had no right making the decision you made – was wrong?

How did I feel?

After the meeting with my neurologist, I asked myself those questions but went deeper than feelings. I finally realised most of my pain had been caused not by my decision or the reactions I received, but through my search for external validation. The less support I had and the more backlash I faced, the harder I searched for that validation. I searched everywhere, including in places that probably weren't mentally helpful for me.

We push people to dark places when we can't accept them for their decisions. We push them to places that offer less support but more hatred and anger. These are the only places that have the door open for support; they are located in the extremes of personality where people end up becoming something worse than what we think they are.

Luckily for me, and because of all my mindset training, I spent a lot of isolated time trying not to go to these places because I knew that where I really needed to go was 'within'.

From within is where I first made that decision. What I was at that time, and what I remain as is the only person who knows my body and what's best for it. I am the only person who lives in my body, day in and day out. The only one who knows its ailments, its traumas and its feelings of elation and freedom – and what it takes to achieve those. I'm the only one who knows how my body moves, operates and responds because I've spent so many years in my body, I've learned how to read each signal and I've honed the skill of listening to what it is telling me.

I'm the only person who lives my exact life experience each day. I'm the one who has found the ways to improve my physical and mental health. I'm the one who's dealt with the trauma of knowing there is still a serious medical issue in my background that needs to be treated with respect. I've spent a long time finding what works for me and my body, and how I can live the most effective, safe and enjoyable way I can and that doesn't harm me or others.

As a part of that, I couldn't make the decision to be vaccinated – and that should've been enough.

It was enough, though – for me. Deep in my soul, I knew it was enough because I knew me. I knew my body. I knew my intuitive reaction to being told I should be vaccinated – an instant hard NO.

In my quietest moments, my moments of reflective thought, I could happily sit with my decision and know it was the right one for me. But in the light of day, amid the bombardment of news and other people's opinions, I couldn't reconcile that I didn't have validation from someone other than myself. It was a constant head versus heart (or gut, in this case) battle to feel and know that I made the right decision, all while sitting in the chatter of my brain as I struggled to justify it.

And finally, I had that validation.

So many of us rely on external validation – our society is set up that way. Waiting for someone to love you. For someone to recognise your talents. Buy your product. Promote you and your salary within the workplace. Waiting for people to choose you to spend quality friendship time with. Our systems of marketing in a commercial society prey on our need for external validation. In neon flashing lights, they loudly say, "Feel like you are missing something in your life? This will help you get there."

We tell ourselves that when we receive that external validation, things will be better. Our lives will improve and, initially, they often do albeit on a smaller scale. A simple thank you really does go a long way. But, even when we receive validation, the primary need of our body and mind is to feel acceptance at a much deeper level – one that can only exist within ourselves.

Waiting for validation is a lonely process. It is a journey fraught with the fear of having made the wrong decision or feelings of not being enough. Not having validation sent me on a dark soul-destroying journey where I had to confront whether I could accept what my stance meant for my place in society, and whether I would be comfortable standing out on my own as exposed as I was. It was a journey of imposter syndrome, and feeling my words weren't strong enough in my explanations. A journey of incredible self-doubt and a desire to lock myself away so I didn't have to explain why I wanted the right to live my life the way I chose. It was a journey where my whole body and soul knew I'd made a thoughtfully calculated and correct decision, but couldn't understand why I was still struggling with my self-acceptance of it. Dredging up my past and explaining my story to provide an answer was also painful and something that I didn't want to do. My daily quest for further knowledge – as I watched the media's opinion, spoke to those closest to me for their honest thoughts, and scrolled through the social media posts of those who screamed loudest in my feed – felt like an attempt to self-sabotage my intuitive decision.

A quest for external validation doesn't do much towards honouring one's journey. However, I needed to do that. I needed to respect my story of how I got here. It didn't belong to anyone else. No-one else had lived my life. But this quest also made me research every little thing I could about Covid, about those who got vaccinated and those who didn't, the statistics, the stories of those with my condition and whether vaccination was triggering previous illness or whether getting Covid was making it worse.

It would be easy to say that I made a decision, put everything I believed in behind it and stuck to my guns, unable to be swayed. I wish that were true. But it wasn't. I second-guessed myself every single day. I had to keep reminding myself of a past that, previously, I had been comfortable to forget. I engaged in a constant dark reminiscing of how sick I had been to remind myself how much worse I would be if that happened again.

In those brief moments when I wasn't searching for external validation, I thought about what it meant to make this decision. I was choosing to be one of the four per cent here in Melbourne. I was choosing a better life for me over a forced vaccination in the most locked-down city in the world with the most strict vaccine mandates in Australia. It meant I was about to become a person who may lose quite a lot in the process, all while knowing it was worth it to not return to the life I quite literally almost lost all those years ago.

I had to trust my gut and push away the thoughts of whether I'd made the right decision. I had to fight against the narrative – so viciously presented in mainstream media, a place I once called home – that the four per cent were crazy conspiracy theorists. They didn't wear tin foil hats. They had valid reasons. They believe in personal choice, like we all should. Sometimes, despite facts presented to the contrary, that personal choice will save an individual's life.

If you can put your arguments aside for just one day, you might read this and entertain the idea of curiously attempting to understand a different perspective. Because that is what it is. A different perspective from a different person who has lived a different life from yours. A person who has different traumas, a different skill-set, a different upbringing and a different experience of the medical system, yet has done the very best for herself like we should all aim to do. Someone who does not care what your choice was as long as you chose it for yourself, are comfortable with it and were not forced into it. I am not fighting this fight for myself but for each person who wants autonomy over their body and life choices.

This is important, now more than ever. I battled writing this book. I had moments of knowing I needed to get it off my chest while also feeling like no-one would care. I've published it sitting, somewhat awkwardly, balancing between the two. I'm also worried I've left it too late.

Yet, there is one very current concern in our modern society that stands out as a reason for this book's continued relevance.

A word or two about AI

As we head into a post-Covid world, we are now facing the fast-paced and somewhat uncontrolled emergence of Artificial Intelligence, which, among other things, has the potential to make all our decisions.

We are an algorithm's choice away from living a completely different life based on what is presented to us. Lines have been drawn. Sides have been picked. Divisiveness is the new black. We are a one-sided disciple of a war we don't even know we're in, one that's being masqueraded before us as woke ideology.

Never has it been more important to do what you know is best for you.

If nothing else, right now is the time to work on our feelings, work on our triggers, address the issues we've ignored, use our voices to say what needs to be said, talk to people we trust and contemplate their perspectives, and let our gut be the first thing to respond to any situation.

In an AI world, we are definitely going to need to listen to that deep intuitive response. It may not be a perfect succinct answer just yet, but it will set us on the right path of questions to ask to continue to hone its skill. In an AI world, music is not going to be made by musicians anymore, and books are not going to be written by authors. We will continue to have perspectives shoved down our throats based on the algorithm of the last article we read. We are not going to know what information is true and what is not. There is going to be a very calculated and deliberate attempt to make us think in a certain way if we haven't already survived the various attempts currently made by the modern world. We are going to be told we are free but we won't be. The only thing we are going to have is our gut response. It will be enough but we will need to learn to pay attention to what it is telling us. Everything we will need to survive this period is within us already, as long as we don't ignore it. As long as we treat it with respect.

Trust yourself.

But do the work first.

And ask yourself, if we succumb to allowing AI to dictate all our decisions, who (or what) will validate them?

Your turn

How much do I feel I currently need validation and how important is it to me? What points about Covid do I need validated? Did I make my decisions about Covid without the need to be validated? Was it a gut response? What other questions do you have about validation?

The lessons

Lesson 2: Connection

> *In order for me to satisfy my instinctive human need for connection to something greater than myself, my brain constantly searched for a way of validating my own argument.*

Connection is at the core of validation. It is the brain's way of trying to satisfy a biological need. In our society, connection presents itself as a fundamental need for a sense of community. We all search for connection. It's in our biology.

At its core, connection is a biological process that has existed for millions of years. Yet, our ever-changing brain forms habits and beliefs that often need to be questioned and, at times, do little to serve our best interests. Therefore we find ourselves searching for concepts, such as validation, as a way to fill our connection void.

Our brains are amazing organs that adapt to change and repetition of what we do in our world. What we say internally to ourselves, and externally to an audience, matters to our brain. It changes who we are and what we think. Our biology still wants to connect, so we link our ever-evolving thoughts to this biological desire, mistaking our brain simply wanting us to fit in for genuine connection. Would our biology largely remain intact if our society reflected the needs of a human more genuinely?

We have changed how we function in society so much that we now feel more isolated than ever before, and have a greater desire to reach out and connect with anything at all. These days, we are not as community-minded as nature intended. Society dictates that jobs don't need people. Social media gives a false sense of community, without a physical connection. The heavy and fast-paced elements of life mean we are more likely to want to retreat from the very connections that are vital to make – to our community, our surrounding environment and to our inner self.

What we need most is to return to a more natural flow of life, rather than continuing to push against it as hard as we do.

We all see the flow-on effects of a lack of connection. The great Johann Hari talks about the breakdown of members in a damaged society through lack of connection, leading to people resorting to drugs, alcohol and other addictions.[19] Maybe these people tired of trying to be someone they were not in a world that told them who they had to be. Then, without unconditional love, and without any support for exactly who they were, they found themselves trying to find it, or trying to forget they need it, in a bottle or a needle.

Negative examples can also be seen in lifestyle choices that have you trying to keep up with the Jones family, no matter the cost and sometimes to extremes, like joining a cult. The spectrum of connection and need for community spreads across all things, positive and negative. It includes anything, from belonging to a particular sporting club or religious group to joining an online chat group filled with misogyny and hate.

Some connections are helpful and beneficial, catering towards our best interests and creating lifelong friends who share in our journey. However, it's important to remember that not all our interests and values will be the same and that's okay.

Other connections are not helpful but are needed by the individual. This side of the desire for connection breeds a need for continual validation from people with whom we initially had a shared interest, although we may not agree when it comes to other things, including ways they live their life.

At times, some people can't distinguish between the two and mould their beliefs and opinions around the person they are seeking validation from; in the process, they become someone they are not.

It is the latter situation that often stops us from just being 'us', and presents as the feeling of always trying to fit in, instead of trying to feel at peace within yourself.

Experiences like the lockdown and vaccine debates mean everyone is forced to pick a side, whether we want to or not. There is often no room for acceptance of a different opinion. People feel they need to join the chorus of support or risk looking like they sit on the other side and deserve to be ridiculed. This is exactly what happened in Melbourne – and throughout Australia – and bred hate and division. In fact, it is still a topic that discourages any independent thought.

People will do almost anything to not be on the outer. In an extreme case of 'pick a side', like what we saw during the pandemic, people will belittle, defame and destroy any person they don't understand for the sake of showing their allegiance to their 'community'. If that doesn't work, they will medicate, eat and drink themselves into not feeling the pain of disconnect.

Despite what it looks like, however, it is not society that we are disconnected from – it is ourselves. Each one of us can become so disconnected from our own true selves that we can't find our like-minded community because we simply don't know who we really are.

We all have examples of that awkward social circle; the one where we've tried to be just like everyone else. We've pretended to enjoy the same things. Laughed at the same jokes that we don't understand or, worse, know are completely inappropriate. But we don't want to stand out. We don't want to be different. Why? Because we are concerned about what people will think of us. We don't want to be the one that's 'not liked' or 'unfriended'. We don't want to be different. We worry we'll be shunned, talked about and cast out.

In putting up with everything and being quiet, we believe we'll cause no waves. The thing is, we do. And quite energetically at that. We aren't being our true selves. We aren't vibrating at our own frequency.

What's more, when we don't appear as 'ourselves', we also don't enable those who are exactly like our 'genuine selves' to find us – and join our true community. We create further disconnect. A disconnect from ourselves and a disconnect from other like-minded individuals who otherwise would have found us.

Either way, we are often shunned. We are awkward to be around because we're not real, we're pretending. We're not honest with who we want to be because we're trying to be someone else. Regardless of our efforts, we then don't fit in because it never feels natural. You give yourself away too easily. You're in your head too much. Nothing feels in flow.

In that search for validation, for connectedness and for a community that thinks like us, we often lose ourselves and our own unique persona because we get so caught up in finally fitting in that we excuse the other things we might not like or might not agree with. We seem to forget that we can share views and experiences with others but not everything we do in our life will be – or needs to be – exactly as that person does. There will be opposing ideas and different choices at times, and that is okay. It's a very natural part of life.

We are frequently guilty of painting people with the same brush stroke because they have a certain opinion on one issue. This does not leave room to experience each person as they are. Our situation, where a choice about vaccines became an argument where people were expected to show what side they are on, we allowed that to tarnish a person's character. Instead of putting aside one difference, we let that one thing dictate an entire relationship going forward. We labelled people. Put people in the same category as criminals. Drew a hard line down the centre, and placed each person on either the good or bad side. We decided, based on one factor, that a person deserved our attention, our friendship and to be heard – or they didn't. The 'anyone who thinks differently belongs in the bin' attitude lacks real understanding of the complex nature of human beings, and the beauty that none of us are the same.

People either belonged or they didn't.

Think about memes like 'He's a ten but …'. What does that say about the people who post these? They can't accept difference. They can't be curious about the reason or life experience behind the decision. Maybe one genuine conversation to understand might make the person realise they don't even know why they hold their fixed opinion that is challenging to you. Maybe they are willing to look at your point of view. Maybe it will be a topic where you can easily agree to disagree.

As humans, we actually need relationships with people who challenge us and make us grow. No-one ever learned anything new from their closest group that parrots what they themselves already do.

You grow from difference.

You grow from experiencing what you don't already know.

You grow from trying something new.

You grow from mistakes and the life lessons that come with them. But in the age of social media and everything being recorded, people are either too scared to find themselves through making mistakes, or they make the biggest ones they can for social acceptance.

It's all about connection and belonging.

I accept there are some non-negotiables, and that we need to have the same values to feel comfortable in another's presence – but you don't need to agree on absolutely everything.

I'm saddened that a power-grabbing Premier, a mandate-creating government and a drama-fuelled media allowed the debate on vaccinations to be a non-negotiable that pitted otherwise good human beings against one another without any room for discussion. It broke down genuinely needed connections within our society at a time when people would have benefited more from discussing the heavy changes in their life. Shunning these people was actively encouraged. We were expected to remind them they were making the wrong choice. We had to treat them like they deserved to be outcast from society. In doing all of this, our society has created a pathway where all topics, post-Covid, are now being approached in this manner. We are drawing a line in the sand for every issue that should be a discussion. It's a dangerous way forward for our country.

Along with a lack of communication, the support for picking a side over every issue means we have become more divisive. The referendum on The Voice to Parliament, which side of a war we are on and gender identity discussions have created such a divide in our community. I have been told who is in favour and who is not. I have heard grabs on TV and read quotes on Twitter that slam 'stupid people' on each side of those debates.

I don't believe, however, that any of us have actually heard an explanation about what it means to be on either side. What will change? What will stay the same? What is the middle ground? Media and government platforms serve to further segregate society on these issues.

People need discussion. We need a space for respectful conversation. We need to have our concerns listened to. We need to express ourselves without judgement. We can't expect people to 'put up and shut up'. We can't be 'a hard no' to every change, nor can we promote change without any genuine discussion and consultation with those it directly affects.

We all need to stop wanting to be the loudest voice, stop trying to outdo each other, and come together to understand. I want decisions that affect real change for the diverse people in our society but I have no idea whether many of the current discussions will grant that because they're arguments rather than respectful discussions. We are simply hearing the loudest voices. The only thing that seems to matter is what side you are on and whether that makes you a good person or not.

The media and the government have a responsibility here to stop flaming the division that exists in our society. If you make people hate each other, they become much easier to control. Much easier to sell to. Their opinions are much easier to shape.

Do you want that for yourself? Do you want to be easy to control? Do you want decisions made for you?

It's your life. Demand control. Stop waiting to be told what to do and how to think. Maybe then you'll find the self-respect you long for. And then, you will find genuine connection.

Your turn

Who are you? Where do you need to connect? What have you sacrificed for mere validation? Do you believe you've tried to become something you are not to find your people?

Lesson 3: Fear

Some days, I have what I call a 'Beetlejuice reaction', where I fear if I say TN out loud or mention its existence too many times, it's going to reoccur. I know that's not possible but it's the story my brain is choosing to play at this time, and I'm in a constant struggle to not let it win this round. It's like an opponent who's happily cheating and I've got to read it the rules.

Fear is both the biggest motivator and will stop you in your tracks at the same time.

It demands a decision because you have no choice, yet renders it impossible to make one.

Fear will tell you you're not ready and will force you to move forward at the same time.

It will see you take a brilliant leap of faith, and also make a stupid and rash judgement, usually in the same day.

Fear will make you find your people and, in the same breath, it will cause you to lose them.

In the last three-plus years, that which was motivated by fear for you, and motivated by fear for me were likely to be opposite sides of the same issue. There was no definitive right and wrong, only what was right for me, and what was right for you.

Where the motivation of fear really makes a difference is whether the fear is negatively motivating you, or positively motivating you. It's all about whether fear has made you reactive or contemplative. Whether the fear has forced you to instantly react, or respectively respond. Whether fear allowed you to sit, listen and process, and then make a thought-out decision, or whether it forced you to choose the fear you cared about more.

Consider fear in terms of the vaccine situation. What made people make their choices? The fear of dying? The fear of having a different opinion to the social norm? The fear of losing money, housing or your way of life? Perhaps it was the fear of having a pre-existing medical condition, that you had worked so hard to prevent recurring, only to have the potential of it coming back?

Or, simply, maybe it was the fear of making the wrong choice.

Emotions are instant and singular. They emit a bodily response from us but the reasons for them are complex – past traumas, current environment, or even the different stories we tell ourselves.

Telling this story is hard for me. It's not because I'm afraid of your opinion. It's quite the opposite actually – I'm afraid of the pressure of being your saviour.

A friend once asked me if I was afraid of failing or of succeeding. I chose the latter. If people read this and disagree with me, I already know I'm strong enough to handle it. It is the responses I want that I have a hard relationship with: you found something in it and tell me it changed your life: it made you stop and think; it made you reach out and apologise to someone whose opinions destroyed your relationship. I don't know how to take these responses or what they mean.

Am I on a pedestal and I'm scared I'm going to fall off?

What if the next move in my life is less than desirable, leading me to take a bit of time off, go through a reset or experience a period of depression? Will you say, "Well, what was the point?"

Do I now have to be the voice of reason all the time? I'm happy doing these things for me, but I don't know how to do it for anyone else.

I realised something when I finally got my letter from my neurologist – whether she had or hadn't supported me, I was going to continue doing what I did anyway. If she didn't agree with me or support me, I would've still trusted I'd made the right decision for myself because the fear of the alternative was so strong.

I was happy to stay in the very strangely survivalist comfort zone I'd created for myself with its boundaries of who I spoke to and who I shared my information with. But when she did support me, I knew it was a big deal when she said, "I don't know if I could have done it." It was my invitation to step out of my comfort zone. To finally be me. To show up for myself and know I was right.

I didn't know if I was ready to do that. I knew the truth. I knew I wasn't wrong. And I was scared because I also knew I'd have to do something about it.

For two-and-a-half years, I was scared. I wanted to find others like me and hear their stories. I wanted to tell them they weren't crazy. That they weren't alone. That they had every right to be angry or sad, and every right to defend themselves. The thing was, I couldn't say it out loud myself. I sat in a hidey-hole of anonymity for my own mental health.

I knew I was justified in my response, so as time went on I started to wonder how I could deal with not sticking up for myself further. How could I justify hiding when I hadn't needed to? I realised that if someone else out there, just like me, needed a story of support to read, then it was me who had to write it.

My vulnerable honesty scares the shit out of me, which is how I knew I needed to do it.

The last three-plus years have not been fair. Far from it. Along with the others in the four per cent, I've been made to feel ashamed, feel 'less than', feel crazy. The mandates told us that we didn't deserve a place in society. We didn't deserve to earn money or make a living.

And for what?

For an illness that didn't care in the end if you were vaccinated or not.

For an illness that still spread to your nan despite the government stance that you'd be saving her.

For an illness that, over time, will continue to take a toll on the health system and be responsible for a far-too-early death count from suicide, isolation, loneliness, lack of adequate care in nursing homes, familial separation, unhealthy coping mechanisms, body shame, depression, anxiety, eating disorders, social anxiety, heart attack and neurological conditions.

For an illness that was responsible for loss of business, loss of identity, loss of meaning and loss of purpose for so many. For an illness whose biggest legacy is that it created fear.

Your turn

I chose to shift my fear and funnel my feelings of anger, frustration, distrust and so on into this book. Ask yourself this – what did fear do for you over this time? Was it helpful? What were you really afraid of? What were your feelings? How did you use them? How and where have you channelled them?

The Four Per Cent

Lesson 4: Reality versus truth – our need to be right

> *"The only thing that's going to stop us getting locally acquired cases going forward, we know is vaccination ... We can't stop it. The only way to stop it is vaccination." (Former Queensland Chief Health Officer and current Queensland Governor, Dr Jeanette Young, 7 October 2021.)*[20]

The reality is the above statement was given during the Covid pandemic. The truth may be that early data suggested this to be the case and the former Queensland Chief Health Officer wanted to provide an encouraging statement in support of vaccination. This statement would now be deemed incorrect.

Is our human need to be right a motivation or a deterrent? Does it help us discover the wonders of the world or hinder us from ever being able to immerse ourselves in a true experience? Do we listen to contemplate or listen to respond? Do we really care to hear what anyone else thinks or are we just waiting to beat our chests to the sound of our own voices?

And what version of 'right' is it? Our right? Someone else's right?

There is reality and then there is the truth. Each person's truth is different. You can explain your opinion until your heart is content and then contradict yourself in the very next sentence. But for you, both are true and this is where the complexity lies because truth is only true to us. Truth is not reality, although is often confused as such.

Our search for the truth is what drives some to greatness and others to an early grave. On both sides, there are people who believe they need to have an opinion either way.

But do we?

Opinions are like arseholes, everyone has one. Your opinion will be made up from your unique existence and can be both right and wrong for each individual.

The reality of a situation might be that a child is dead because they were riding their bike and struck by a drunk driver. The truth of the situation, however, will be different for each person involved.

Reality is fact. Truth is a version of the same event, and told by the person who knows the story. Truth varies depending on how empathetic to the situation the teller is.

The driver's truth might be that they had one drink. Their truth is that they are currently on medication, which may have increased the alcohol reading to 0.05. The child was riding on the footpath and decided to cross the road without looking. The truth is that it could have been any driver that hit that child.

The truth of the newspaper headline is that a dangerous drunk driver killed a happy child.

The truth for the reader will be determined by the photos that accompany the report, the parts that are put in or left out and who is interviewed. All are based on what sells best.

The truth to the parents will be 'who could do this to our perfect child?'

The truth to the child's neighbour will be that it was an accident waiting to happen as the child had no control and was often engaging in hooligan behaviour.

The truth to the driver's family will be that their upstanding, model father who volunteers for the Red Cross and has three children of his own that he takes to basketball on the weekend is not reckless. He was a victim of circumstance. He accepts he was wrong. That he broke the law and the reality of what has happened has left him deeply devastated.

All versions are the truth for each individual, yet the reality is a child is dead and a driver who was over the limit is responsible.

I used driving as an example because I was a driving instructor and I had a range of students who were eager to learn, along with the ones who ask why they have to stop when it's not their time to give way.

Personal responsibility is the greatest lesson I can teach them as an instructor. It doesn't matter if they do everything right – if they can, in the moment, eliminate the possibility of an accident that may occur if someone else does something wrong, they should also do that. Many will argue and ask why. Maybe at their age, they already feel like they have the weight of this crazy world on their shoulders, and why can't everyone just do the right thing?

Unfortunately, the right thing is not the same for every person.

As incredibly wrong as it may seem, the right thing for one driver might be to get to work on time, which is something others can't control as they can only prepare themselves. In doing so, and teaching others self-accountability, maybe there will be less people trying to get to work on time and more people accepting that their driving has an impact on everyone around them, not just themselves.

You are not too important.

Everyone needs to be somewhere. It's your responsibility to wake up earlier. It's not everyone else's responsibility to get out of your way.

Any person with a school-aged child wants to keep them safe, so will appreciate my methodology in this way of teaching. They will want their child to have personal responsibility instead of just arguing that they shouldn't have to do it.

Think back to anything you have said to your children during the pandemic that doesn't fit with personal responsibility. Have you just told them to do what you say because you say so? Did you become a 'Dan Andrews' in your own loungeroom? Did you encourage them to follow the rules and get vaccinated because all their friends were? Or did you listen to their concerns and questions?

Did it bother you that they just went along with what everyone else did, or did they actually come to you to discuss what they thought about it? And if they didn't, why not?

The Four Per Cent

Are you presenting yourself as someone who is approachable? Someone to talk to about whatever they need to get off their chest? I know I'd rather someone come to me for honest discussion than go to someone I'm not sure would listen in the way that is needed.

Are you encouraging your children to have independent thought or are you shutting them down?

Are you encouraging yourself to have independent thoughts or is something shutting you down?

You can still own your truth without blocking out reality.

Your turn

Can you listen without also wanting to be heard? Did levels of communication you worked so hard to instil into your relationships with your children, friends and family slide when you were faced with the biggest health care decision you've had to date?

The Four Per Cent

Lesson 5: Having an opinion

Many people – strangers, friends, colleagues – seemed uncomfortable knowing I had a different opinion. They'd grunt and shut down the conversation. They'd flat-out tell me I was wrong. Or they'd make noises about me not understanding and then send through articles in an attempt to arm me with more information in the hope I'd change my mind.

We all fall for it. Ten friends post a black square on their timeline and even though you agree with the sentiment, you don't feel the need to virtue signal because you know it won't really do anything for the cause. All you know you need to do is just keep being a fair, reasonable person who treats all people of all denominations the same as you always have. You are comfortable with that.

By the next day, 350 of your social media friends, plus businesses you follow, have posted a black square. You start questioning if people will think you are racist if you don't, so even though in your gut you know you don't need to and it's not going to make a difference, you post that black square too.

Are you sending money to America to fight the cause? No.

Do you still live in a country where a lot of how you live your free life is still surrounded by the oppression of your own country's First Nations Peoples? Yes.

Have you personally tried to change that locally? Not enough.

On many occasions, I have felt the need to virtue signal due to peer pressure. Of course I have, I am only human and to be human is to be perfectly imperfect. Virtue signalling on social media is the new peer pressure of the school yard.

Do I care about 'black lives matter'? Yes, of course I do.

Do I think a black square is the best way to show that? No.

Did I do it anyway? Yes.

In my weaker moments, I suffer peer pressure as much as the next person. But consider this simple statement:

You do not have to have an opinion about everything.

Half the time you don't really have an opinion; you are just venting anger, frustration or fear. You're pissed off and you think directing what is really going on into something that is currently topical will make you feel better – but it won't.

Woke culture feeds into this.

I believe it is possible to have conversations about the past that we didn't like. It's possible to have real conversations about the things that are wrong, and that, sadly, we cannot change without completely eradicating history.

Do we need to apologise for the Stolen Generation? Yes.

Should we be erecting monuments of First Nations leaders and having a voice to parliament? In the right context, and if it facilitates real change, then absolutely.

Do we need to pull down every single statue of people who, years later, were revealed to have done something wrong? No. Hear me out …

Can we change what we think about that statue or change the plaque to show that we can learn from what the past has told us? Yes.

So many kids have depression and anxiety these days and this will continue to grow with the amount of data being stored on every single thing they have ever done. Many of us in the millennial and older brackets are grateful that each embarrassing moment of our early years, where we were just growing and learning, is not still available for the world to go back on at any time. Parents are told to explain the complexities of social media and sharing things that one day will come back to haunt them.

So why do we then set up this precedent of cancelling the past and giving a false sense of security in a digital world that you can take shit back?

You can't!

It happened! Growth is the only thing to learn from it.

Why are you setting your kids up to believe that they don't need to be worried about their consequences because years down the track they can just delete it and it won't matter? And what does it do? It shuts down the conversations about child trafficking and sexual abuse to whomever it applies.

You can dislike Michael Jackson but still dance to 'Smooth Criminal'. You can dislike Kevin Spacey but still agree he was fucking brilliant as Keyser Söze. In ten years' time, no-one will remember who Kevin Spacey is when all his movies come off Netflix and he is not allowed to be spoken about. Everyone will conveniently forget they liked him – all except his victims and no-one will sympathise with them, we won't hear their stories, we will disempower them. No-one will care for the people whose stories they don't know. Can't we say this person was an exceptional actor or singer; however, this is a dark part of their story. Can't we use it to understand that because we like one part of someone doesn't mean they are to be idolised for everything. To delete them is to delete all that they are, not just the bad but the good as well.

In our society where everything is available online, are you raising your child to think they are only one social media mistake away from being cancelled? How do they then truly go out and experience life the way it was intended – by learning through trial and error. By making mistakes. By owning their decisions and understanding accountability.

How do we then applaud people like Grace Tame and Brittany Higgins if we cancel the people they fought so hard to tell their stories about?

And, in the age of social media, do you pretend you didn't watch *House of Cards*. Do you pretend there is no video of you dancing to Michael Jackson at your wedding?

By doing all that, you are saying, "This didn't happen!" Isn't that the original problem we have? Not having the hurt acknowledge.

If you want accountable politicians, start living in a society that expects people to listen, considerately respond, and take action to apologise, instead of reacting to defend themselves and ignoring the part they played.

We all have Dan and his minions saying, "I don't remember." As discussed earlier, this is why The Voice to Parliament didn't get up. People were told they didn't need to know. They didn't need to discuss it. It didn't affect them. Just do the right thing.

Even in my first job, I was told to ask questions. "Don't just pretend you know and if you make a mistake own it."

To take it back to basics, why do we write a pros and cons list? We write this list to find a more weighted side to help with our argument or decision – because there are two sides, every fucking time. Even in a situation where it doesn't feel like there is, there is something to be learned about how the other side got to where they are to make that dreadful decision.

We tell kids, "Don't do what everyone else does. You can still like so-and-so even though everyone else is mean to them."

We all have good and bad in us.

We all have opinions that have changed over time.

We all have the right to say we don't know enough about a situation and don't feel a need to pick a side.

Your turn

Have you subjected yourself to cancel culture, pressured or otherwise, just to agree with everyone else?

The Four Per Cent

Lesson 6: The mass contradiction

Everyone had a reason to break the rules. Personally, in hindsight, I wish I'd broken more.

Oh, the irony of the loudest social media voices then being the biggest contradictors of their own opinions.

I heard 'Stay inside, you're going to kill everyone', 'I've had my jab – didn't get my free tin foil hat', 'Everyone is acting like lockdown is the equivalent of being in Afghanistan' and 'Djokovic must die' from the same voices that also said, 'Roe vs Wade is a failure of our own right to bodily autonomy' and 'Let all refugees in despite vax status because they have a reason to break our rules'.

We all know those people. I deleted some for their complete disrespect of the human race and for displaying a truly horrible side to themselves that hurt me as I saw it play out. I continued to follow others for the sheer ironic comic relief that they wouldn't have even been able to see in themselves.

The 'I just said the exact opposite when it was an issue I cared about. Now I'm on the other side of the fence because the content is slightly different despite the argument still being the same' crew. These are also the same people who were saying, 'Stay inside if you have even sat in the same train carriage as someone carrying Covid, despite there only being one recorded case in Victoria right now'. And the same people who, less than twelve months later, said, 'I'm going Christmas shopping at Chadstone on 21 December and I'm going to post all about it on my social media, despite the fact that my child's boyfriend who visits many times currently has Covid. The rules are now different and I prioritise having my purchases more than saving lives this year, despite the fact there are currently 60,000 cases in Victoria'.

The 'I yelled at you out a car window when you were walking solo up a large hill on the edge of a walking trail that no-one else was on because your mask was only covering your mouth and not your nose. God forbid you were trying to breathe a year ago when there was only four cases in my suburb, but now that there are 1,654 cases in that suburb, I'm not wearing my mask in Woolworths or on the crowded train to the footy anymore cause I did my time and I got my vaxes and have also already had Covid three times so I no longer believe I have to actively try and stop the spread' people.

The 'you will do as I say' Premier who was fined for not wearing a mask but it's okay because I'll blame it on the parents drinking coffee in the playgrounds and the devastated businesses for daring to bring takeaway to the locked-down locals. Said Premier was also publicly shamed for slamming what was never a pub crawl and a street party out the front of a pub that was actually closed.[21]

Trying to say, "I know we all don't like this situation," without a sympathetic bone in his body.

He didn't get it. It was his attitude we didn't like. Being treated like children, told to stay at home, and punished when all you do is say 'I don't remember whose decision hotel quarantine was' – that was what we didn't like. It wasn't 'the situation' at all.

There were so many mass contradictions, where do we start?

Perhaps we start with your concern that you will die from Covid – a respiratory illness – because I'm not vaccinated, while you stand 1.4 metres from me – smoking.

Or perhaps you were concerned you would die from Covid if I passed within 1.4 metres of you – yet you drink excessively, or eat yourself into a grave daily, or take copious amounts of drugs, prescription or otherwise, to mask a variety of health issues that you have, despite never giving any thought to changing anything about your lifestyle, nutrition, exercise, work stressors or your general environment in order to make yourself better.

How about the daily advertisements that, for two years, said, 'Don't leave home for more than an hour, don't touch loved ones, stay isolated.'. Not once did one tell you what you could do. If it is your responsibility to do the right thing, then it is also your responsibility to do the right thing for your health. Eat well, exercise, serve your community.

How about we fear people into social isolation and loneliness, while cutting sunlight exposure, nature exposure, and removing them from their community and social support – but remember to expect them to just pick up and get on with it and never talk about it again.

Here's the thing about trauma – if you don't discuss it, trauma never leaves. You can't just forget it. You need to process it. You can't learn from it and move past it if your solution is not to do anything.

Let's drug everything with medication – everyone spends so much time not wanting to feel anything, but then being upset when they can't feel anything. You need to feel pain to feel joy or how do you know the difference?

And the ultimate mass contradiction? Saying you hate your life while doing nothing to actively change it. Stop expecting someone else to fix you. You have to do the work yourself. How about I take responsibility for protecting your health once you actually step up and take responsibility for improving it first?

Your turn

How can I show up for myself? Where do I still believe someone else will need to change before my life will be better?

The lessons

Lesson 7: Guilt as motivation

It has annoyed me that the Covid pandemic and subsequent debate on vaccination brought to the surface things I believed I was past. But it did teach me that it's not about getting to a stage where I never have to think about past traumas and decisions – it's about feeling comfortable when these are discussed.

I subscribe to a school of thought that says 'the only truly self-motivated people fit into three categories: no choice, terrified but supported, and narcissistic or just plain ignorant'.

Those with no choice have nothing and no-one. They have to act and they possibly already know the life they will live if they don't.

The terrified are fucking terrified but luckily have enough social support to carry them through the 'did I make the right decision?' and 'am I coming across as a wanker?' stages. They'll survive but will always be uncomfortable thanks to imposter syndrome. However, each time they act, they'll get better and be more resilient to failure. They'll eventually let go of fear and learn to trust the process.

The narcissists are motivated because they don't think about anything else that doesn't pertain to their own conquest. Most are completely ignorant to how their decisions affect anyone else, or they simply don't care.

I have operated in all three of these categories in my life, and maybe that's the journey we all go on. I was a very self-motivated child because I was ignorant or simply not old enough to be affected by the world around me yet. When I was very unwell and suffering poorly at the hands of the medical system, I had no choice. And now, in writing this book, I'm basically just fucking terrified while simultaneously having many of those 'If not now, then when? If not me, then who?' moments. I know I'll instantly regret those thoughts as soon as I hit publish. And I'm aware that I'll then ride the ups and downs of that decision for the next five years. But now in my forties, my ability to care is declining with age.

What's my point?

Never feel bad for making the decisions you did because odds are you were not intrinsically motivated to change your own life but motivated by guilt.

Do it for grandma.

That didn't work for me because it's been fifteen years since the last of my grandparents were alive.

Do it for the immunocompromised.

I will sound like the most selfish person in the world, but during this time my father was diagnosed with prostate cancer. My mother is an insulin-dependent diabetic. Not once did I believe I was putting either of them at risk. It was more of a risk for me to get vaccinated.

I was right.

Funnily enough, my mother, my father and I are the only three people in my immediate family, most of my extended family and my friends who have never had the spicy cough. My parents are both in their seventies and have seen a lot of me over the last three years during their trips to Melbourne for various hospital visits, specialist appointments and family celebrations, and when I've travelled to see them I've never once worn a mask in their house. And only once, when I actually had a runny nose, did I test to make sure I was not carrying the danger while in their presence.

I would like to take this opportunity to say my parents were, and are, fully supportive of my decision. Their only concern was if I could handle being shunned by the rest of the world. I guess only the people standing in the room and hearing me screaming in agony as I was being wheeled in for my brain surgery in 2010 could wholeheartedly agree that I was likely to be in more danger than they would ever be.

I had a strong enough reason to want to make my decision for myself. The hard thing is that many other people didn't have that personal reason. They made their decision because 'it was the right thing to do for others'. If they were unsure, they were guilted into doing it.

There was a lot of talk about people who get Botox or take recreational drugs being seen as ridiculous if they refused vaccination. They already put stuff they know is dangerous into their bodies, therefore they have no valid argument for contesting the safety of the vaccines – right?

The thing is that each of those people were still allowed to make decisions about their life. I even applaud those who did get vaccinated because they weighed up the risk for themselves and decided it was best for them too. I just had to hope they could see I also weighed up my options and had the right to decide that, for my individual situation, vaccination wasn't the best option.

It didn't work that way.

Making that firm decision purely for myself was seen as selfish and that is where people felt justified in telling me I was wrong. They didn't have to listen to my point of view because it was a selfish one.

There are not many people who can explain the fear of TN. Recently, however, I watched interviews and read articles about Australian celebrity, Denise Drysdale, who confirmed her TN diagnosis in late 2021.[22] 'Ding Dong', as she is affectionately known, detailed what her life had become in various interviews on TV and in magazines, using the words 'nightmare', 'agonising pain' and 'fear'.

Having a celebrity telling these stories in the media at around the same time I was locked down for my decision sent my sense of self-preservation into overdrive. Suffering one of the most painful conditions known to man versus the possibility of catching Covid? It was a no-brainer.

I had a strong, personal reason to oppose vaccination but I should never have needed one. None of us should have needed one. My neurologist wrote that I should never have been forced and that the decision should always have been mine. Surely she can't have been the only one saying that?

Any opinion other than 'vaccination is the only way' was dismissed for such a long time that we are only just starting to see one-off interviews from people who are finally starting to speak out.

Dr Aseem Malhotra is a UK cardiologist who is currently travelling the globe, discussing the right for freedom of choice in the healthcare space and issuing his own concerns about patients developing cardiac-related events after a Covid vaccination.[23] He rarely gets mentioned in the mainstream media.

Australia's own pandemic voice, Dr Nick Coatsworth, has also been ridiculed for his new stance that questions the effectiveness of lockdowns and extreme government measures.[24]

Dr Kerryn Phelps openly discussed the issues associated with complications from the vaccine that affected both her and her wife.[25] Those interviews were a one-day news cycle. If you didn't catch them that day, you probably have no idea they even exist.

In each of these situations, we have medical professionals who took a vaccine either by choice or guilt, or to adhere to government policy. Now they are using their voice to state that maybe it wasn't necessary or that the strict rules around it didn't achieve the result we hoped for. Still – with the exception of Dr Malhotra whose full opinion is only available if you follow his social media – their wording toes the party line.

Why are these perspectives one-off and one day only? Why don't they get the mass media attention? We had a press conference about case numbers and vaccination rates every single day. Where is the follow-up? These are the real topics that need to be discussed.

Perhaps the guilt of realising they were wrong weighs heavily on the media organisations for their role in the pandemic response.

Your turn

Who did you make your decision for – yourself or others? What are some questions you think still need to be answered?

The lessons

Lesson 8: Better leadership

> *The biggest mental battle going forward will be that of the righteous who attached so much of their identity to 'supporting vaccination' that they couldn't see the science for what it was. Now that a relevant period of time has elapsed to actually see the effectiveness of the vaccines, the data shows that it wasn't the saviour it claimed to be. The fact that the government's own wording changed to the vaccines just offering 'good protection' proves that.*

If you look up a dictionary definition of science, you will see that science is the process of learning about the natural world through observation and experimentation. Scientific knowledge is developed over time. It is based on outcomes, measured against statistics and, in this instance, tested on populations. Those who fund that science can have an impact on how information is presented. Those who benefit from its findings can have an impact on whether that information is shared.

Were our leaders, and others we trusted to have the answers, aware of this when they were telling us every day to 'trust the science'? Did we question why we were trusting the 'facts' on a topic that was still being observed, and vaccine that was still in an experimental stage?

What I learned from this period was that 'unprecedented times' didn't mean 'let's experiment to see what works because this has never happened before'. It didn't mean 'let's make some big decisions but keep an open mind to the fact we may need to backtrack'. What it meant was 'we are going to make harsh rules and enforce mandates without the opportunity for review. If the science shows a lack of effectiveness as it develops over time, we are going to double down, bring in the riot squad and shift the focus away from coming up with a better solution and on to the people who won't comply. We are then going to actively encourage everyone else to demonise those people as the common denominator to pin all their frustrations on.'

The health implications affected everyone. It's no wonder people became so angry and lost. They didn't know what they thought anymore and, if they did know, they didn't have the ability to voice it. The mental implications are still felt and will continue to be felt until the situation is addressed – not just by those who were against vaccination, suffered ridicule, had no support and lacked a voice, but from those who genuinely just wanted to ask questions and arm themselves with more information.

Many people now refuse to accept the science and the data – the very 'facts' they used to throw in our faces. The government could be seen to be assisting in that denial by not being forthcoming with relevant statistics, and directing our focus to how hard it was to make a decision. Rather than saying they accept vaccination actually didn't work the way they thought it would, they have stopped recording further data and started to destroy records. Why? Because the reality doesn't fit with the narrative they presented.

Those who were in decision-making appointments at the time of the Covid response are suddenly retiring or changing roles, and as such, are no longer needing to be accountable.

The media is not helping either. Why aren't they asking questions as to why we're not covering the new data, the current stats and the accurate presentation of the science? I would be – if I was still there. And where is the follow-up on the biggest period of change in most people's lives? Oops – they can't do a story on something they followed and then fired their own staff for, can they? It would be an HR – sorry, 'People and Culture' – nightmare. (A name-change doesn't mean you actually care about them any more or less than you did previously.)

There are always innocent victims on both sides of any war. People that suffer when those in power want to justify their actions.

How I craved for a leader who would come out and say, 'This is a genuinely hard time and although we are currently responding based on the best advice we have, we will review these decisions as time passes. We will take concerns on board and find ways to address them. We can debate what's working and what isn't – after all, science is observation and experimentation.'

Instead, we had leaders who may as well have said, 'You will do what you are told or there will be consequences. I will use the long arm of the law to instil fear into every moment of your life. We will fine you when you don't comply. You will find a way to best deal with it or I'll come down on you like a tonne of bricks. I'll state you are solely responsible for putting everyone's health at risk. You want to push me, just watch how far I'll go outside of actual health advice just to stroke my ego. You want to make your own decisions? No income for you. You want to visit friends? I'll hold a press conference to state I wouldn't be letting an unvaccinated person into my house.'

Many studies, and a shit-load of Netflix documentaries, exist about the abuse of power. We had a daily display of that here in Melbourne at each press conference with a long focus on a Covid-zero approach.

If we were to ask that same leader today what they now think of the unvaccinated, would they still be scared of them? It was a big call to say they wouldn't be letting them into their house. Are they, and others like them, genuinely scared of the unvaccinated, or are they just sticking with that same opinion because they can't handle being wrong? Was that inflammatory language even necessary? Vaccinated people still got Covid and they still passed it on. The unvaccinated were not responsible for that.

Experts make mistakes especially in unprecedented times. Own it. The negative opinion towards the unvaccinated minority has not changed. It should have – especially with science now pointing to the fact that vaccination wasn't the be-all and end-all to eradicate this virus. The persecuted few present an uncomfortable truth that no-one wants to speak about. It was never their fault.

How much pain, loss of life, loss of finances and security will it take for politicians to admit they were wrong?

A quick look at examples of leadership throughout history may give us the unfortunate answer. The Holocaust. The Stolen Generation. Thalidomide. Where are the leaders who owned the mistakes that affected these people?

Any definition of leadership you care to look up will include words like courage, integrity, empathy, self-awareness, respect and gratitude.

How many of those qualities were displayed during Covid?

Why do we still call these people 'leaders'?

Sometimes recognition is all that is required to move on; for someone to say, "I was wrong and I'm sorry. I didn't mean to hurt you." What strength is there in waiting till it's a forgotten topic. That is cowardice. That is not owning your part in the story.

Your turn

What would real leadership have looked like for you during Covid? Can you be a leader now? How can you change this narrative going forward?

The lessons

Lesson 9: Where did the stress on the hospital system come from?

"... what a hide you have, what a ridiculous position is that when you're going to put health staff at risk, and when you get sick you're going to expect to come into hospital and get paid for by taxpayers." (Brad Hazzard – Former Minister for Health and Medical Research of New South Wales, 29 July 2021)[26]

We have a health system in crisis and Covid didn't start it. Covid merely highlighted it.

Our approach to so-called health in a Western society leaves a lot to be desired. A Western medical approach diagnoses and treats patients based on their current symptoms. In traditional practices worldwide, such as Chinese medicine and Ayurveda, health is considered to be a state of balance and to adequately get to the root cause of illness, the whole person – their lifestyle, nutrition, mental wellbeing, and even the presentation of their hair, skin and nails – tells the story of a lack of balance within that individual.

Traditional medicine looks to restore balance, thus restoring health.

Western medicine defines a single disease within the body and aims to eradicate its symptoms, but rarely the cause.

In 2023, it is stated that one in two people will develop cancer. It's snuck into the discourse of modern life as 'that's just how it is'. We focus our attention on donating money to cancer charities and it's used to hopefully find a cure plus develop a new range of treatment options.

I don't know about you but I grew up being told prevention is better than cure. Our Western medicine system is void of prevention.

It's a system that says, 'Let's not focus on what caused it; let's just try to fix it at the end or at the very least make it a little nicer process to deal with.'

Not only does this stress the hospital system, it puts the responsibility for health solely on to the doctors, nurses and other medical practitioners and scientists forced to deal and come up with solutions for it.

Traditional medical practitioners believe they aren't doing their jobs properly if you don't make improvements in your overall health. Western medicine, on the other hand, focuses on finding ways to have you live with that imbalance permanently. A cycle of appointments and prescriptions allow us to survive, assisting with the occasional maintenance, instead of empowering us to take control.

Where is the self-accountability for the way we choose to live our lives? Where is the public discourse about the things that should be paramount in society to encourage health? Western society simply promotes a medical system that can drug us up to forget the problem, rather than encouraging us to live a happier, healthier life.

Western medical practices are dangerous for our hospital system, but more detrimental is our society's acceptance that we can't help ourselves. We identify as whatever disease we may have.

People love to identify: I am a St Kilda supporter; I am a doctor; I suffer from depression.

And each identity gives us an excuse for our behaviour: I'll be upset for three weeks after a loss for my team; I'll shut down any responses to your questions with my ego alone; I cannot and never will be able to do what you're asking of me as I'm comfortable hiding behind my diagnosis without learning to work with it.

We'll use all of the above as an excuse to never better ourselves, attempt to learn or try anything we find hard.

A diagnosis does help by giving us somewhere to start. They help steer us in the right direction. Get us the help we need. Provide a framework for treatment and to teach ourselves and others different approaches to better support us.

But our diagnosis is not who we are. A diagnosis doesn't define us, yet our society suggests it does. Sometimes we don't need to find a reason for our crazy, it just is.

Creating thousands of different groups of diagnoses and identifying markers leads to more division and less inclusion. Let people be exactly who they are. The more wonderfully different people in the world, the better the world will be.

These days, everyone is on a spectrum. Life is a spectrum. How we experience it is a spectrum based on our beliefs, our environment and the stories we tell ourselves.

From a medical perspective a diagnosis creates excuses for the often simple fact that we've moved so far away from our natural state by the way we live, eat and socialise. If we got back to being connected with our community and environment, who knows … maybe these random, once rare conditions wouldn't be so popular.

Can you explain why an increasing number of seven-year-old girls are now going through puberty? It's not evolution. It's a lack of focus on nutrition and the provision of an optimal environment for growing bodies so as not to stress their developing hormones for healthy living. It's the same reason so many people struggle with infertility, or why we have so many depressed and confused teenagers not knowing who they are. We don't change the plant – we fix the environment it is growing in.

Herein lies the concern of the modern divided world. We have an environment that is toxic and not being addressed. We have people getting sick within that environment. We have big corporations benefiting from it staying that way, a medical system that doesn't address the root cause and makes a simple diagnosis based on the current upward trend, and a society that not only accepts it but campaigns against anyone asking questions as to how we got here.

Don't hide behind your diagnosis.

Don't tell me I don't understand – because I do.

Find a way to work with it. Find a way to be comfortable being you. A chemical imbalance is just that – an imbalance. It's not a marker of permanence. The environment needs to change. I've seen the proof with my own eyes. I've worked in wellness centres around the world and seen people who can't get any more help in the medical system in their country; they've been given the news that this is now their fate. I've seen them then spend three months changing their diet, exercising and being surrounded by positive people in nature's daily playground. And I've watched them as they completely change their lives. Some suddenly get pregnant when they'd been told they were infertile. Some have their first pain-free period after being diagnosed with endometriosis. Some put their body into remission from cancer. Some suddenly lose weight they've never been able to shift in their life. Hell, I've even done it myself.

You can get help. You may require a lot more than the person next to you but that's okay. You have to believe it is possible and keep searching for the answers. The biggest factor, however, is yourself. Are you willing for it to get hard before it gets better? Are you willing to find people that support you? Or are you content to surround yourself with people who will constantly allow you your excuses and feel sorry for you all the time? Only you will be responsible if you wake up in ten years in the exact same position, telling yourself the same bullshit about how you can't lose weight or be happy because of the cards you have been dealt.

Medication is a godsend for some people. It has been a godsend for me during my most painful moments of TN but I never wanted to stay on medication forever because I was very aware of the changes in my own physical and mental body while on them. Not all of the changes were good. I needed the initial assistance but I also looked for ways to improve the situation. In hindsight, taking a breath and realising my current world didn't support my illness would have helped. If someone had pointed that out, I hope I'd have listened. But I probably wouldn't have. I'd accepted I had my illness but I refused to let it define me. I missed the part where I should also treat it with respect and not just assume I could continue to live the way I was.

We use medications to such an extent we never feel the warning signs in our body or the varying emotions of the human mind. People need help to address these things, to talk about them, and to get them out of our skin. The body really does keep the score. You become stiff, withdrawn, nervous and anxious. You just want to scream out loud. It can be seen in the way you hold your head, the way you walk, the lines on your face or in the circles under the eyes. We easily catch the colds and flus going around. We get inflammation around the stomach and joints, and overall pain through the body.

Don't ignore the signs. Don't push them down. They won't stop bothering you. You won't forget about them eventually. That shit lives under your skin. Deal with it. Process it. Move through it. Don't mask it by taking pills, partying it away, excessive eating, drinking or exercising. Don't bury yourself in work or someone else's problems. Make this commitment now to change how you deal with things, and to express your feelings at the time. As my favourite poem, 'The Invitation' by Oriah Mountain Dreamer (2006) asks, *I want to know what sustains you from the inside when all else falls away?*[27] Could you honestly answer that? Take this opportunity to learn who you are and what you are made of. Don't let the lengths you go to stop feeling the pain take away all that you really are, or what you could be.

What we need to learn is that we can't continue down this path. If we want to blame Covid for the stress on the hospital system, we made it worse during this time by allowing people to blame others – the unvaccinated – for their illness rather than the state they were already in, prior to the pandemic.

There has been a mass move towards 'root causes medicine'. Thank fuck, quite frankly. It needs to be pushed harder. Why would you want to stay with a system that puts a bandaid over everything, only to rip it off years later and realise it's made it worse.

There's also a number of contradictions, such as eating better and not using plastic straws to protect the environment, while at the same time pumping a fuck-load of chemicals into our bodies to stop feeling sick.

Your body is a healing machine. You look after your animals, plants and children, but you don't look after yourself. You medicate to not feel the actual responses your body gives you to tell you when it's in trouble. Years of depression medication or painkillers and then, wow, I have cancer or vision problems or something else I didn't see coming because I've literally drugged myself stupid to stop feeling anything unpleasant. Those unpleasant feelings are your body's warning sign that you need maintenance. That you need to try something different. They may even save your life, yet our medical system tries to shut them off to control the body we've lived in all our life.

Get vulnerable with the unpleasantness of life. Be honest with people and say, "I've just lowered my dose of medication and I'm going to do my best this week. Can you please assist in a gentle transition?"

We spend so much time hiding who we really are and what we really feel that by the time we speak, act and play, we are a programmed version of ourselves designed to be something for everyone else, usually people we don't even care about that much – our bosses, colleagues and neighbours. We are rarely who we are. Nobody needs to find themselves. We need to be unafraid to just be ourselves in the situation and life we are currently in. If it doesn't fit, have the strength to change it.

The Four Per Cent

Your turn

What's one small change you can make to improve your own health?

The lessons

Lesson 10: Staying well

Sluggishness, the inflammation, the upset gut health and the general lack of enjoyment in life means I'm at a place that I don't want to be and I'm hoping soon I can chill on the trauma-reacting and start getting some of my general health back. I know what sits on the other side of where I am currently. I've been there a few times. The path is just a little dimmer right now and that's okay. I'll take a torch and search for it when I'm ready.

Staying well when you have a serious affliction is hard. It's a daily task to show up for yourself. And it's a daily battle to keep away the memories of how bad it can get. Trying to eat better, not indulging as much but also living life are essential. It's about understanding when the mental health benefits of a social gathering are more important than obsessing over whether there will be natural and unprocessed food available.

The other side of the coin is trying to not become disgruntled with society. You shouldn't need to choose. Being able to stay healthy should be something that is easy for people to do. It shouldn't be affected by a cost of living crisis, or wrongly advertised because a powerful company is the financial donor of a supposed health label.

We should be living in a city where fresh fruits and vegetables that are not sprayed with unhealthy chemicals should be easy to obtain every day. Where we encourage incidental movement by walking to public transport or riding a bike to work. Where our bosses do not encourage us to sit all day in an often toxic windowless environment without taking a lunch break, just to make a large corporation richer. We shouldn't need to prioritise an extra hour's money over quality time with loved ones. We should have friends and a community close to us without the need to spend more time sitting in a vehicle and requiring a whole day of our time just to socialise with friends who were priced out of the local area.

The businesses that never sleep provide us with nothing more than fast food and support for our unhealthy habits. They remind us of when we have been time poor, disorganised, lacking in options or just plain bored. They are there to facilitate our downfall.

The devices that never sleep remind us we are but a cog in the wheel of a society built on profit and that, as a consumer of life, you can be bought by anything it chooses to advertise. The device holds your data so it knows when to play with your emotions. It's like a narcissistic friend showing fake support for the sake of getting something in return. We are being used 24/7 but this is cleverly marketed as help, all while failing to write a real disclaimer about the losses of in-person social connections and your sense of worth.

It also shouldn't be something you have to justify needing or explain the way that best works for you to obtain it. You do you. As long as it is for your own good and doesn't affect others find your way to own your story.

Taking control of your life is not easy. It can be so tempting to get someone or something else to do it for you. Have this pill to fix the pain rather than address what's causing it. Eat this shit food rather than take the time and spend the money on a healthier alternative. Drink this alcohol rather than remember and process the pain or have a hard conversation. Smoke this so you can step out of this reality for a while as it gets too uncomfortable.

I get it. I too do some of these things when I'm not ready but I learned a very harsh lesson about ignoring pain – it doesn't go away. You need to learn to live with it. You need to process it. You need to question the way you respond to it and you need to strive to learn and make better decisions around your dealings with it. It does get easier but you need to ask yourself the hard questions: What do I need right now? How can I take control of my life?

The lesson we may have all learned during this pandemic was that all the things we hadn't dealt with in our lives presented themselves in the pressure cooker environment we then found ourselves in. It may have felt like Covid set off a lot of these unpleasantries but it really just bought them to the surface.

It is our responsibility to keep ourselves well.

A word about negativity

How does a negative mindset affect your health?

It bores a hole in your soul. Being constantly reactive affects you more than you think. People don't actually need you to point out that they are wrong. Just as a child falls several times before they learn to walk, we will all make mistakes until we learn the lessons we need.

Being positive all the time to the extent of not allowing yourself to feel other emotions is also not helpful. What is helpful is catching your negative mindset and taking a moment to address whether you could present your current thought or reaction to yourself once again with more constructive language.

Your turn

How can you redirect a negative mindset? What are some ways to speak to yourself and others with more curiosity and kindness? How can you help yourself stay well in mind and body?

The Four Per Cent

Lesson 11: Less entitlement, more love

The entitlement of being able to tell people what to do, how to feel, what they should care about continued when it was decided that the only thing that would get us out of lockdown was a vaccine. No ability for discussion just pick a side and don't look the other way.

Being unapologetically you and having others around you respect your decision to live the way you wish is priceless. Knowing that one difference of opinion won't sway people from appreciating that you still deserve love and respect is everything. This is why we love pets, or come back to those who always have our backs in times of trouble. There is a magical healing moment when you arrive home after all the shit that's happened for the day. You may have made tough decisions. You may have been the arsehole at times. But you have that one somebody – human or not – that only cares that you are home and they want to shower you with love. It heals us. It gives us a sense of worth. It tells us that everything is going to be okay. We may have had a bad day but we are not bad people. There's no judgement, just pure unconditional love.

The human variety may then move on to asking the questions needed to shift our mood. In these moments, we don't need the black-and-white answer. We need the compassion, the unconditional love that we don't receive from the majority out there in the world.

Why?

Everything is sold to us as a competition. We have to be better. We have to work harder. We can't make mistakes. We have to improve daily.

What we need is to be human and to be given the space to do that.

A great quote I often refer to in my coaching is 'the moments we believe we need more self-discipline, we often need more self-love'.

Wouldn't it be a much nicer place to live if we could get this from the people around us every day, instead of relying on an often non-human to provide the support we need on our return home.

We all need to sit in our feelings. Give ourselves time to feel what we were up against in that moment. Let the brain tick over before it decides where it goes from here. Animals give us the ability to do that. We don't have to feel ashamed. We don't have to answer to anyone. What if we all had people around us who just listened and then asked, "Do you want to vent or do you want advice?" Our Covid experience could have been so different. You never know what a conversation can do. Those who are no longer with us may just have been.

Yet, people often believe they have to give you their opinion of your situation – and often it's not asked for. Sometimes we just need to speak the thoughts in our head out loud before they make sense to us. We may simply need to shift the feelings associated with it. What all of us need is unconditional love and support.

You don't have to agree but it helps if you listen.

Your turn

How can you better show up for others? Is there a current situation where someone might just need you to listen? Can you listen without responding? Give an example where you believe you should have done that previously.

The Four Per Cent

Lesson 12: What to trust

You may be wondering what is left for you to really trust.
The answer – yourself.

Your body knows what it needs to focus on. Your thoughts take you there in moments of reflection. You know what your vices are.

Every single thing about us – what we enjoy, what we experience, what we believe in, right, wrong, good, bad – elicits a response in our gut. We may not always process it in the moment but deep down we know what our soul craves. We know what upsets the very root of our core values. We know when we are inspired, and when we are acting from a place of love or hate.

We spend so much time caring about whether we are doing the right thing by everyone else, we don't find time to worry about what feels right to us. It doesn't matter, anyway, because we just want to fit in. We want to be like the people we're all most drawn to – those who live freely. We spend hours trying to understand why others naturally like these people – and we try to be just like them.

It's all about energy. When you stand in your own strength, and respond in a way that, deep down in your soul, you know is right, you will live a life that is best aligned to who you are destined to be.

Think about your happiest times. Your defining moments. These times are where you've fostered creativity, community, connection and inspiration. Why, then, do we work so hard to gain more status? Why do we strive for individual achievements? Why do we aim to impress the people that won't benefit most from our efforts? Why do we not do everything for ourselves?

Over the last three-and-a-half years, during the pandemic, our society somehow rose to a huge level of hatred and self-righteousness – and this is how. We don't care about each other. We care about being right. We care about being on the popular side.

I love people who are unapologetically themselves. It takes courage. It's a level of courage I find in the deep recesses of my soul and, when I find it, I have to take action in that moment otherwise I'd never do it.

To take that action, I have to break down all of my conditioning and reassess everything I've ever been told. I have to get past every environmental, schooling, and life-in-general construct that has been thrown at me and just believe and push myself to do it. It's not easy, but fuck it's worth it.

My motto in life has always been 'don't be boring'. I hate boring people. That sounds harsh and I know I should find a new way to describe it but I can't stand people who just do what everyone else does. I admit, I do find myself in those positions from time to time, and I am most annoyed with myself when I do.

You may think that taking time to reflect on your actions and thought processes, along with eating well, getting sunlight and exercising is a bunch of hippy shit. If only it were that easy, right?

Well, it's not that fucking easy – and that's the point. Making a change is hard!

It's all hard.

Actually listening to your intuition is hard.

Being unapologetically who you are is hard.

Motivating yourself is hard.

Dealing with your self-limiting beliefs is hard.

Working past childhood trauma instead of burying your head in the sand while you continue to repeat the same patterns over and over again is fucking hard.

You have time – just use that four hours you spent scrolling social media today – but you live in an oppressed society that prides itself on showing you exactly who you should be, what you should like, what you should buy, who you should fuck and what is considered successful. So, you follow those rules.

Did it work?

Are you happy?

We are all perfectly flawed individuals – fucking embrace it. So what if you have ADHD. Maybe you don't. Maybe you just live in a society that expects an unattainable level of keeping up. Perhaps you're in a constant state of fight or flight. Perhaps you're depressed. Perhaps you live in a society that you are so over. Perhaps you're in a job you hate. Perhaps your daily running around is to run away from your own life. What if you actually sat for a moment and thought, 'Do I actually like this life or am I constantly trying to distract myself from it?'

I'm not actually trying to live in the moment. I'm too busy worrying about what I've done previously and about what is coming up. Now I'm documenting it to prove to other people that I enjoy it – and I worry about that too. None of it is a judgement. I also do all of these things. I am no different but I'm here to ask, "Have we all had enough?"

Surely it's time for all of us to fight back against where this is going.

Have we learned the lesson yet?

Have we tapped into our intuition?

Think of the moments that shape us – disasters, floods, fires … even the first year of Covid. We find a way to cope. We are inspired by the decency of other humans. We are inspired by the underdogs, impressed by those who didn't stand a chance. We love attending festivals or sporting events for the energy of a crowd of people gathering together for a shared love.

Take a moment to think about the last time you thought, 'Wow!'

When was the last time you were genuinely surprised?

Deep down, we love difference. We love something outside the box. We all wait for the next big thing without realising someone has to be that first brave person to decide they're going to do it.

Be yourself.

Don't be afraid.

Listen to that intuition. Trust it.

Be you. Unapologetically you.

The Four Per Cent

Your turn

How can I trust my true self?

The lessons

Lesson 13: Everyone has a different experience of this time

> *Resilience isn't something you are born with, it is something you learn. The more you put yourself in difficult situations, the more you can handle them. By the time I boarded my flight to Thailand on 8 January 2023, I had been in a few difficult situations. This one was pretty bad; at the time I thought it was my last chance to get into the country. It was stressful but I repeated a mantra to myself, over and over and over again, 'Everything is going to be okay. You've got this.' And I did.*

Have you had a difficult experience? Have you suffered trauma?

There will be those who say that a year of your life is hardly comparable to Nazi Germany, the war in Ukraine, living in Gaza or fleeing Afghanistan. In a podcast with Jay Shetty, Dr Gabor Mate explains this perfectly when he talks about the use of the word 'trauma', and how people say they have experienced trauma when, really, what they have endured is a difficult experience.[28] He points out though that it still matters to who feels it.

The lesson of resilience can only be built through hard experiences. And the moving part in all this is relativity.

Think back to your school years. Do you remember thinking it was the end of the world when your friend stopped talking to you? You thought everyone hated you and there was no way you were ever setting foot in that schoolyard again. A great trauma.

Even further back, as a young child, you might throw a tantrum, screaming and crying for hours on the floor if you got the red balloon and not the blue one. Again, it's one of life's greatest traumas.

For many people, the experience of Covid lockdown was the worst thing they had ever been through. The hardest thing for them was the fact that everyone was going through it, and people handled it differently. There is nothing that can make you feel more inadequate than the greatest stress to your body so far being compared to how every other person is dealing with it at the same time. There would have been others who were having a similar experience and some who relished in the quiet time at home. There may have been a number of people who didn't enjoy it much but had survived worse before and so tried to make the best of it. Yet, the length and repetitiveness got them in the end. And there were those who were quick to judge others, saying, "It's not a war zone, get over yourself."

For students, the Covid pandemic absolutely uprooted their lives. Cast your mind back to those moments in life where friends were everything. Where being in school with your friends and having them pay attention to you shows your life has meaning. Imagine being forced to stay at home, unable to see any of them. Add to this the online issues, where all the teasing, backstabbing and suffering continues online while you're stuck in the house with nowhere to go.

This was absolutely the end of the world for some of these students, and it needs to be validated. It was a horrible time. It was a sad time. It was a frustrating time – and all the emotions in between. Being told that at least you could still talk to your friends didn't cut it. Two years is a long time in those formative years, under the age of eighteen, where you make connections that help form the person you become. That time was lost for them. It doesn't matter that it wasn't a war zone – for many of them, it was the hardest thing they'd faced.

How many parents put themselves into their child's shoes at that age, remembering how big a deal school problems were? How many said, "Get over it, it's not that big a deal," before turning back to their own issues?

It's not just the parents who need to be aware of doing this – we all do. This is where we fall over as a society. If we found ourselves able to manage the situation and it wasn't the end of the world for us, then everyone else must feel that way too. Why on earth are people acting like it's the fucking end of the world? It's fine. I'm fine. Why aren't you? Because for some people it was not fine. And not having their feelings validated in any way meant it was literally the end of their world. Not being able to express the emotions they held over that time, unable to find it within themselves to deal with their emotions, and feeling weak if they asked for help – it meant they chose instead to end it all. It was the only thing they felt they had left in their control.

We've all heard the saying, 'be nice because you don't know what someone else is going through'. This is the epitome of that saying. We tell children that it's okay for them to learn at their own pace. It's okay if they are not good at sport. It doesn't matter if they are brilliant at maths or not. It's okay to be different. Then we chastise the adults who are too emotional, too rigid, too upfront … too whatever. We isolate them for the very differences that make each person the beautiful individuals they are.

During the pandemic, we'd all hear comments like "Why can't they just mask up?", "Why do they have to be so difficult?" and "I've lost my job; they only have to work from home. What's their problem?" Why don't we just ask that person? Why do we find it so easy to bitch and make judgements about people, but so hard to actually ask the question we want answered?

If you start every conversation in your life by asking a question without judgement – a question for the sake of listening to the answer, rather than to prove someone wrong – fifty per cent of the world's problems would be sorted. If you hear every question as a person asking for genuine insight, instead of reacting like your ego is being threatened, guess what? We've solved the remaining fifty per cent.

I invite you to do yourself a favour and read up on *Nonviolent Communication* by Marshall B Rosenberg.[29] You may need to let go of your old ways but the strategies in this book will change your relationships. It will stop you harbouring anger and believing that people should know why you are upset without you just telling them. Most importantly, it will change the way you talk to yourself.

I can't talk, though. I spent two years not telling people that I wasn't vaxed because I feared judgement.

The lesson is simple. Everyone has a different experience of this time. All experiences are valid.

Your turn

Any last thoughts on your experience of dealing with the pandemic years?

The Four Per Cent

Part 4:

Where to from here?

When I started writing this book, my hope was that by the end of the book you would appreciate that each person, even with their differing views, has a lot of similarities to you.

Each of us are humans with thoughts and feelings. We all express emotions. We are all individuals with our own experience of the world and are just trying to exist among a variety of people who we are connected to in more ways than we care to acknowledge. Your story of this time is just as important as the next person's, which is why I wanted you to have the opportunity to share your experiences and express your feelings each time I shared and expressed mine. Despite how it may have felt in the moment, we were in this pandemic together.

Collectively, I think we can all agree that none of us will ever get those three or so years back. So let's get past it. If you have fully participated in this experience, by responding to the questions and prompts, maybe you will no longer feel that same frustration when the word 'Covid' is mentioned. If you haven't, go back when you are ready and start to answer those questions. Maybe you won't have to address it over and over again if you say what you believe needs to be said.

We need to talk about this, as a society and as individuals. Everything around this topic is so heavy and angry, and it cuts deep. You may never get the apology you think you need. You may never be understood in the way you want. What you can do is clear the pain out of your own mind and forge a new path forward. Finally put Covid behind you. Carrying the associated trauma around with you will not help. We all need to move past this period in our lives and start to shape who we want to be in the future. Do we want to continue to be divided? Or do we want a genuine sense of community?

I have told you exactly how I feel and have given you the space to share your own feelings about the same topics. The written word is my story, the white space is yours. Our stories can be different but true to both of us. We can empathise that we both struggled but maybe for different reasons. Some people will have lost friends and family to Covid. Some people will have lost those with no strength to hold on during harsh lockdowns. Some people would have lost their job, financial security and way of life, their very identity. Some people would have lost their socialisation skills, many friends and a list of things that are equally important to them. Each and every one of these things matters to the person who has lost it. Don't rob yourself and others of the chance to feel and process this major time in our lives.

As the world continues on this path of division, our social media feeds get louder and louder. People who would consider themselves caring, accepting and 'here for others' are sharing inflammatory posts, demanding someone be held responsible.

Awareness is one thing. When used correctly, it can show us how we can make a difference. Demanding attention and telling people to pick a side is another. One gets the compassionate response you are after, the other inflames the opposing side and then no-one can see the situation for what it truly is. The division continues.

We all have these posters in our social media feeds. We can summarise most of their content. Knee-jerk reactions trying to get people to care about what they believe is the biggest issue of the time in a style of simply shoving it in their faces and being outraged that others aren't talking about it. Living in the drama of every single one of these moments. Never using them to start a conversation but always using them as a way to show where their allegiances lie in the debate. Demonstrating they have no room for discussion on the topic and simply assuming that making people feel stupid if they disagree is the way they will get people to listen.

These posts definitely do not marry with the supportive person the poster thinks they are. They show so much of their own unprocessed emotion publicly but expect others to do the work on themselves. They never realise that the people saying nothing are, for the most part, actually the ones doing the work to better understand the situation. Or they're simply just holding the light for others, rather than adding to the heaviness. They are proving that there is still beauty to be had in the world.

Another thing we can agree on is that none of us asked for the pandemic and we all had to find a way to survive. Each person's way was different; it was either right for them or the only way they knew how. Why not use the lessons that can be learned from this shared experience as a start towards becoming less divided? You don't need to prove you are right; you need to live what is right for you without deliberately hurting others in the process. You need to learn from your mistakes and hard experiences in life to ask yourself the question, 'How can I do this better next time?' Your life should not be solely about what you can achieve in the years you have, but how you can also contribute to a better collective experience. Stop thinking about what you want just for yourself and start thinking about what mark you want to leave on the world.

If you want a better society to live in, be a better person in it first. If you want someone to treat you fairly and respectfully, then be a person who demands fairness and respect for yourself and others. If we let Covid be another example of just conveniently forgetting our part in it – how we reacted, how we may have treated others, how we spoke about it publicly, what we shared from the media, and what we wrote in the media – then it becomes just another blight on our history that we don't learn from.

You are not sick of talking about it, you just don't want to because you have learned some truths about who you became during that time. There is a difference. Most people will rely on the narrative: I didn't know better; I did what I was told.

Other people have used that same narrative over the years – the people who fought against women who wanted to vote and work in society, the people who fought against blacks being considered members of the general public, the people who dobbed in the Jewish, the people who bashed homosexuals ... The list goes on; you get my point.

These are not comparisons of what was worse, they are examples of people not communicating respectfully, not expressing their concerns, just choosing a side and flaming the fire of aggression and hatred. It also shows how far it can go when we stay quiet for too long. 'It was a different time' doesn't cut it. It's true that the reality is that it was a different time on the calendar – but a different time of what exactly? Did human beings not have feelings back then? Did people not know how to be nice? Did people not realise when they were being an arsehole? Did they not know how to ask questions and express concerns before making decisions as part of normal adult conversation?

It wasn't a different time, it was a different subject on the current social discourse that was collectively outraged. A different division with which people could vent all their frustrations at the failing of the world. A different narrative that we pinned our victimhood on. Each 'different time' was made up of millions of people who were actually still responsible for themselves and their actions. It was still made up of people who had feelings like fear, guilt and sadness. It was still made up of people who wanted to belong so much that they were too scared to do what was right, so they hid behind what was popular.

I'd love someone from a 'different time' to come along for once and tell me, "I have learned from that experience; I didn't stand up for my fellow human beings. I'm sorry and I am going to live a life now where I don't have to regret something like that ever again."

Instead, we'll get someone who says, "You don't understand. I was forced. You don't know what it was like."

If I don't know, then tell me.

Tell your story of why. I want to hear it. I want to understand. You might find that deep down in that moment, every sense in your body told you how wrong it was but you felt powerless to do anything about it. That's okay, but you need to talk about it. Stop carrying those unaddressed feelings around.

Alternatively, don't tell me at all. Keep believing it's not your story to own – even when you lie awake in the middle of the night, surrounded by your deepest darkest secrets about the person you let yourself become. Continue to do that and watch your body keep the score. Perhaps your mind will join in, finding another topic to vent all your unsaid hurts on.

Have the courage to learn from your experiences. Stop thinking that growth will negatively change your outward persona. Stay curious. Say what needs to be said. Forgive yourself and feel that ache in the pit of your stomach finally ease. Then maybe – just maybe – the external you won't matter anymore because the internal you will be as solid as a rock.

Now, let's look at this from the perspective of owning our part. Let's stop the next cycle of allowing fear of the unknown to divide and dehumanise the next group in society that we don't understand. How about we stop grouping all together? Should we need a title or a different letter of the alphabet or a different pronoun. Maybe we just need to be exactly who we are so we can have genuine discussions about these topics, and what we feel and need in these moments, without letting our emotions take over.

The issue is the expectation not the expression.

Let people show you who they are before you decide for them. We are all different and we should all be proud of that. We should celebrate it. We don't need to fit into anything. We don't need to identify as anything other than ourselves. Let's validate how people feel and ask them what it is they think they need. The more acceptance there is, the less we'll crave it and the more secure each of us will feel within ourselves. That is the true goal of acceptance. The acceptance of self. But you have to understand the work you need to put in to get there.

We believe it's quicker to run away from feelings than it is to sit with them for twenty minutes or so and feel them, respect them, then watch them move on. Worse – we drown our feelings out with various addictions. We ignore them. We push them down. We distract ourselves with quick fixes. We turn the light off on our feelings temporarily and try to pretend they're not there.

But, feelings will make themselves known when they're done being silent. You won't be expecting them. They're like the car we don't have time to service that then breaks down on our holiday. The small comment to our loved one that returns ten years of pent-up rage that barely seems justified because we didn't put the dishwasher on. How much time would we get back if we just addressed each one in the moment? How much space would we create in our heads for the things we need to concentrate on right now?

No wonder we feel overwhelmed all the time! We just let everything sit there and take up space until it can't be hidden anymore. You may think you've dealt with your own shit but do you still find yourself in the same situations over and over again, or five years down the track? Perhaps you're still hoping to get the same things, even though you aren't actually trying for them. Are you still expecting things to happen without going after them? Still telling yourself it 'wasn't the right time' every day? Still putting the happiness of others down to luck, and yours down to the cards you were dealt?

Life is hard for all of us.

When it comes to life, you get out what you put in. Life has challenges. It has absolutely diabolical shit moments. What matters, though, is how you keep adapting to change. Don't be afraid of change – it's growth. Everything in the world grows. Instead, be afraid of not changing. Of staying the same. Of never experiencing more than what you currently know.

Expressing your emotions as they come up, and having those hard conversations with the right people is just a skill. Like any other skill, it needs practice. The more you do it, the less it will frighten you. You'll get better at it, and it will take less time.

Ignoring your feelings only serves to improve the ways in which you currently react. You'll get better at the anger, the frustration, the jumping to conclusions or lumping ten unprocessed situations into the same argument. Your tongue will get more spiteful. Your expectations more negative.

The only way to stop your feelings from moving from mild frustration to complete rage is to practise those hard conversations. Say what you feel. Ask for what you need. We are conditioned to make things so much harder than they need to be. Most of the time there is a simple solution, and although it is sometimes an uncomfortable one it is always about communication.

The world needs us to stop adding stress to our days, lingering thoughts to our heads, illness to our bodies and depression to our souls. The world needs us to take responsibility for our feelings and say how we feel – not how we think others have made us feel. We don't need years of frustration to boil out at the same time. We don't need people or situations living rent-free in our heads. We don't need to relive the same experiences over and over again.

As a friend, listening to others, it is not helpful to perpetuate the cycle by responding, "You're right; it's so unfair!" Simply say, "I hear you," or "I acknowledge your hurt". Then, ask questions to give people back the power to decide where they go from here. Ask them and yourself, "What am I going to do about it?"

By all means, vent. Let it out. Give it the time it needs to be felt. Then, when you're done, take control of it. Don't constantly revisit the same thing over and over, like you have no power. Don't decide it has a hold on you. It doesn't. You just need to find a way. And you will.

Ask for help. There is nothing to be ashamed of when it comes to where you are at and what you don't understand. We all have to start somewhere. You have total control over your life. If you feel like you don't, start finding ways or asking for help from people who can assist you in getting that control back. I'm not going to lie, it will be hard. It will take time, some longer than others. Some will need more help than others but you are the one who needs to do the work. You can share your musings and discuss in kind, but only you can tell your story. Just like only I can tell mine. Don't give away your power to someone else.

Life is a constant journey and happiness is not the destination. Happiness comes from the ability to be truly present in the experiences along your journey. Take a moment to look back at your life and remember all you have contributed, all you have endured, and all you still want to experience. Then go out and continue to live your life accordingly. Appreciate not only the good memories but the lessons learned along the way. Really take a moment to analyse your growth – both good and bad. See how far you've come.

Regularly take stock of where you're at and evaluate whether you're still headed in a direction you're comfortable with. If you're not, make the tough choices. Have the courage to move away from that which no longer serves you. Go back and address situations that still eat you up. Learn the lesson – but don't hold on to the regret. Deal with the feelings that need to be dealt with. Speak to be understood. Listen to understand.

You are the happiness you are looking for.

You are the common denominator in your story.

You are in each of those pure moments of joy you experience in your life.

Where to from here?

Your turn

What is an unprocessed emotion you believe you need to let go of in order to experience your journey truthfully? Describe it.

The Four Per Cent

What else might you start questioning?

Once you've moved your mindset, will there be other things you start to question? Where's the demand for answers with Pfizer?

With all the vitriol around how much we had to do to 'stop the spread' and 'keep everyone else safe', it's interesting that there was no revolt when Pfizer admitted they never tested whether their vaccine stopped Covid transmission before they launched.

But nothing.

Silence.

Where is the media now? They could halt your favourite TV show every day for almost two years at the first sniff of a North Face jacket, but they can't do a story about a multi-billion dollar organisation making false claims about a worldwide mandatory product?

There was and is no attempt to backtrack on such a big issue. There is only hope that it goes away.

Who decides what constitutes fake news?

One little story that slipped through the keeper recently was about the fact-checking algorithm used by Facebook and Instagram during the pandemic. It was touted as an attempt for people to understand what information was real and what was false – but it actually incorrectly labelled a lot of shared information about vaccine concerns, side effects and effectiveness as fake. Even the hashtag 'natural immunity' was banned at that time.

This information – identified by the algorithm as fake – has now been proven to be true.

Google also changed their policy during the pandemic to state that accurate searches would be prioritised.[30] The sites they led us to first would often be news outlets or paid organisations. Less chance of a conspiracy website getting through, perhaps?

What is the difference between conspiracy and fact?

About one year, apparently.

Where is the discussion on other countries who have stopped Covid vaccinations due to concerns for safety?

A bunch of you probably don't know this and, as discussed above, it might be hard to actually look for it on an Australian search engine, but eighteen countries, including Denmark, Germany, France, Ireland, Norway, Italy, Spain and Sweden, halted the use of AstraZeneca in March of 2021 until bodies like the WHO and the European Medicines Agency (EMA) could deem the benefits outweighed the risks after reports of several blood clots.[31]

For context, that's around the time Australia started pushing the use of AstraZeneca.

It is also worth noting – while we are all back travelling overseas with our strongly held views on Covid and vaccines – many of the places you are travelling to did not respond to the pandemic in the same way as Australia. In fact most didn't. Many countries did not enforce mandates. Some tried, but it was proven to be a violation of rights. Some countries had small vaccine uptake, yet no large-scale issues with Covid numbers.

If you found yourself in a country where the consensus was different to Australia's, would you still care to voice your strongly held views?

Where were you on the Djokovic controversy?

While you're thinking about the different experiences had by other countries, so many nations looked at us in disgust over the Novak Djokovic tennis controversy in 2022.[32]

And rightly so.

We deported the world's Number 1 tennis player – and everyone had a very vocal opinion about it.

The following year, Djokovic came back and won the competition, and I totally felt the tears he displayed deep in my soul. The rules for the Australian Open in 2023 – when he won it – were that anyone with Covid could still actually play in the tournament.

What a difference a year makes!

Where to from here?

In 2022, not only did we ban anyone who was not vaccinated from entering the country unless they had an exemption, we let in the unvaccinated Number 1 tennis player on medical grounds. We then questioned him at the airport till all hours of the morning. We allowed him to practise on the courts. Then we locked him in detention. Then we let him out because he was allowed to play. Then we overruled the decision and deported him.

Anyone who thought this was the greatest victory of the Australian Government and proudly supported it on their social media feed with the hashtag #novax should hang their heads in shame.

Then, hang it further if you said nothing the following year and actually watched him win the final.

Djokovic was originally banned from entering Australia for three years. Many people loudly applauded that decision. When he then came back a year later – nothing. Why are you not upset? He was given three years, wasn't he? Weren't you happy about that? Do you just not care anymore? You were so vitriolic in your exclusion of him from the country, why the silence when he gets to enter twelve months later?

Maybe you don't feel that way about him. Maybe you've grown. Maybe you don't feel the same way about the whole pandemic anymore.

But I don't see any of you writing anything!

The diehards will surely have wanted him out. The rest of you probably wanted your free corporate tickets to the final, despite the fact you'd be watching and possibly supporting a person you were almost ready to kill last year, or, at the very least, were happy to see deported.

Many people probably didn't change in the way they felt about him to start with. They would have just found themselves wrapped up in the outrage culture of having to have an opinion about Covid and vaccines and needing to show what side you were on. Now that it's not so popular to have an opinion on these things anymore, suddenly they are very quiet and there's no outrage to be had. However, social media exists forever. Unless you are fortunate enough to be cancelled.

Take a moment to ask yourself why you care to show that you took a side. Aren't you okay with just doing what's important to you and not entering the discussion at all? Are you so worried that people will judge you if you don't show what side you're on?

Maybe this is where you start questioning yourself.

What do you make of the statistics?

Did you know you can look up the Therapeutic Goods Administration (TGA) website yourself to find statistics on the registered side effects of all four Covid vaccines in Australia?[33]

As of 29 Oct 2023, there were 139,654 reports of side effects from Covid vaccinations in *Australia* alone. Nearly 82,000 of these were for Pfizer. Nearly 49,000 for AstraZeneca (which has been discontinued in Australia). These side effects ranged from something as simple as a headache, through to severe complications. The TGA's data even states that in just over 1000 of these cases a death was reported. When presenting these stats, most people will focus on minimising the impact of that data by focusing on the belief that the numbers are largely made up of minor ailments and that the majority of those deaths are not legally confirmed in Australia as being the result of a Covid vaccine.

The interesting fact, however, lies on the other side of the argument – reports of a positive Covid test. When someone said they had Covid, it didn't matter if it was a positive result with no symptoms. It didn't matter if there was a cough but no other ailments. Even in death, it didn't matter whether Covid was the underlying thing that killed them or not. Apparently, because the deceased had tested positive for Covid during their hospital stay for end-of-life care, cancer, diabetes and so on, they were marked as a Covid death. When presenting these stats, most people will focus only on the words *Covid* and *death*.

There can be many ways to read stats depending on what you are trying to prove. Statistically, it can also be said from the 21,000 reported cases of Australian's who either died with or from Covid (as it is now characterised) almost half of these deaths occurred in 2022.[34] Interestingly, the highest number of those deaths were at the start of the year when the unvaccinated were still locked out of society and Australia reached the milestone of having over 95% of the eligible population fully vaccinated. If those people rushed out to get the jab before they were shut out of the vaccinated economy it would also mean they were in the time period of the highest efficacy of the vaccine.

So much for the pandemic of the unvaxed.

These statistics are also the markers that are now determining the discussions around the long-term effects of Covid. If you had Covid, you statistically now have a higher chance of developing a heart attack. If you had Covid, you statistically now have a higher chance of getting a neurological complaint.

Has anyone stopped to think that Covid might just be the wrong common denominator? I could name another possibility – but it would be hard to test that in Australia among only four per cent of the population.

With the rapid development of technology that means drugs and vaccines are able to be developed at lightning speed, and with almost an entire country of people vaccinated and statistics from all over the world to show its effectiveness or otherwise, now could be the time to really get the information we need to help our society. Do you trust who it comes from?

How to move forward

Where are we now?

We're angry, lonely and disconnected. At the very least, we're hurting to some degree.

We're walking around in our everyday lives like individual balls of emotion; each one ready to explode at an undisclosed time and place. There are less pleasantries. No-one has time, and no-one can be bothered wasting their energy in a society where others don't care about us anyway.

We're coiled up, waiting to be offended so we can lash out to soothe our unmet needs.

We're too afraid to ask the questions we need answered for fear of being judged and cancelled. We're being told we need to have an opinion – even about things we don't understand. We've started to find comfort in extremes because we're being made to feel like it's wrong to sit in the middle. An algorithm will decide what we care about and who our real community is.

We're missing true joy and we're looking for it in all the wrong places. We've developed a reliance on external stimuli – prescription medications, mobile phones, gambling, violence, crime, gorging on food, drugs, sex and alcohol – as a way to feel something other than our deepest selves.

We're prioritising possessions over experiences. We value the photos, posts and amount of likes that prove we were somewhere, rather than focusing on developing the memories of actually being in the moment.

We want to prove how right we are about a topic, rather than appreciating our growth as we learn something new, or see it from a different perspective.

We're focusing on jealousy rather than inspiration. Judgement rather than understanding. We're only seeing the few ways we are different, rather than the mountain of evidence we're all the same. We want to have more and be better than the next person, instead of sharing in our human experiences and bringing everyone up around us.

There's a lot more 'every man for himself' these days – and at times, due to the society we live in, it's no wonder. Our remaining trust and empathy is abused by scammers. Everyday necessities are costing almost our whole pay packet, so we're being forced to find cheaper alternatives that don't give money back to our own community. Our food is processed and offers little to no nutritional value. It cannot help shape a healthy growing brain.

Work hours and home life are blurred with the rise in bedroom office spaces. Children are coming home with questions about the world; wanting answers we don't believe they're ready for at their age.

Our living situations are often insular, locked down and disconnected from our neighbours. Basic tasks needed to get us through the day seem more complicated and time-consuming and it's hard to find good help that's cost effective, genuine and available.

We're dragging ourselves through each day, carrying around the weight of our fears and traumas, trying our best to get by – just to get up and do it all again tomorrow.

I do want to help.

But we need to talk about how we got here, who we've become and what it takes to change. We then need to address whether we're directing our fears and concerns at the right people. Most of the time we're not but we're proving we want nothing more than to be heard.

Getting through this book has probably not been an easy task. Probably not an enjoyable or popular one, either. Often the hardest of conversations are the ones that most need to be had.

This book would have presented opinions you don't share. At times, you may have felt heard and could delight in finally being understood. It is likely you had to find a way to put differences aside to make it this far.

I've asked you to find every answer deep within yourself. This is something you may not be ready for today, tomorrow, or ever. It's your responsibility to process that.

This is not a book of comparisons.

It's not about whether someone else's concerns are less than or greater than yours.

It's not about who is doing the right thing or the wrong thing.

It's about the fact we don't discuss the things that need to be said due to the fear of those judgements, and how that eventually affects all of us on a much larger scale.

This is a plea for each and every one of you to realise how connected you are. How similar you are in your fears and happiness in life. I've tried to explain how we all need each other in this life to experience a better one. Being there for others so things don't escalate and people don't start trying to find connections in a group of people who are not supporting their best interests.

We need to talk so previous atrocities in our world won't continue to repeat in a society of individuals feeling downcast and ostracised by their own friends, colleagues and neighbours.

Treat people like they are not worthy and they'll eventually stop trying to be. Without support people will ultimately live up to your worst ideas and opinions of who they could become.

We have to find a way to have genuine respectful conversation – even about the hardest of topics. We don't talk anymore – certainly not about anything important – without judgement and our ego taking over. We need to be able to express exactly what we feel to people who will listen without feeling the need to respond. We need to learn to ask for exactly what we need without the fear of persecution.

We have to train ourselves to listen. Really listen. Listen to understand and hold space for another person without feeling the need to agree or disagree. We have to learn to ask respectful questions that aren't led by our opinion but are more a genuine curiosity for how that person's individual story brought them to this thought. We need to understand a person's right to share their experience, especially if it is different to ours. If you can't comprehend hearing it, imagine what it sounds like going around their head, unaddressed and unprocessed.

First, we have to acknowledge we all need healing. We all have moments in our lives that have shaped us and contributed to the story we tell ourselves about who we are. Some with genuine trauma. Some with uncomfortable experiences that have changed the way we see the world going forward. Trauma and discomfort, and everything on the spectrum in between, matters. Some stories no longer serve us as they have stifled our ability to trust, to accept change, to find strength in our own self and to grow. We need to understand our triggers, heal our traumas and process uncomfortable emotions to be able to understand when we're being genuinely targeted or simply wounded by our past selves.

Your turn

Wait until you're healed, then come back to this section to ask yourself three very important questions. Who do I want to be in this world? How do I want to contribute to it? How can I find my own way and support others to do the same?

Where to from here?

And my point is ...

Who do I think I am to have written this and posed these questions to you?

I've often considered the place I am writing this from. Is it a place of love? Is it a place of concern? Is it a place from which to educate? If I'm honest, I'm writing this from a little of all of these places.

To put it more simply, I just had an overriding feeling that I had a lot to say and it needed to be said, so now I've said it. What happens next is out of my control. It's actually more about what you do with it.

I don't want to know your opinion of me, good or bad. It's not relevant. I want you to ask yourself how facing this topic has made you feel? Which lines felt as if the strokes on the keyboard literally typed across your soul?

If my story angered you because you don't agree I should have been able to make my own choice regarding my own life, then tell me how my decision has directly affected you? I promise you I'm not a threat to your existence.

If my story angered you because you are just as upset by this blight on our history, then tell me who you'll share these thoughts with? Tell me you won't forget your part and you'll move forward with this knowledge to use a louder voice next time. I promise you I'll do the same.

If my story inspired you to be exactly who you are, to find your voice and to live as your truest self, then tell me what sets your heart on fire and show me the work you've done to find those moments. I promise you I won't judge but I may ask respectful questions and together we can come to understand one another.

I can only be me. You can only be you. And that is good enough. For everyone else, it will have to do.

Think less about judging other people's attitudes and opinions, and become more curious about how they came to them. Others may just treat you in kind. I live in this mind and body. You live in yours. No-one else pays the rent.

We all have a little ego. We all have a need for connection. We all have a need to feel accepted. Knowing I've been misunderstood many times, I often think that maybe this book has just been a way to explain myself and what makes me tick, but that can't be it.

I don't care much about who really knows me, at least not now, in my older and wiser years. I enjoy being anonymous with my popular Australian name. I'm not easy to find on socials. I like to live my life never really standing out in a crowd and I like to think that those who I've spent quality time with are as grateful for the experience as I am. I hope they have enjoyed my company. I hope I've made them feel comfortable and safe. I also hope that sometimes I've challenged them and made them think. If they haven't enjoyed their time, then maybe there's something we need to talk about? Was there a lack of communication and understanding, or were we both just having a bad day?

I enjoy meeting a variety of people. I love the experience of learning something new about each one and am always interested in what brings different people joy. I also have days where I don't have the energy for anything other than putting two feet in front of me. If you meet me on those days, I apologise. I promise it is not about you.

For each person I meet, I genuinely hope the best for their lives going forward. If they don't like me or they judge me, I don't feel a need to correct them. I just accept that we're at different places and maybe, in a different time, we'd understand each other more. I rarely put much weight on what others think of me and therefore I'd say I don't care too much about being understood by the general public, or the seven degrees of separation people reading this book.

I have my close friends. That small group of people know who they are. They too have made me think. They've provided much joy and unwavering support, even in the hardest of times. The longest-standing ones have also seen their ups and downs with our relationship as we've all changed so much over the years. They are the people who I have in mind when I write something like this. Have I made them proud? Is this a true representation of who I am? Are they going to call me and say, "Page 57 – who you writing that for? That's not you. I call bullshit!"

If you're in my inner circle, you'll know. You'll know the workings of my mind. You'll know my opinion on most things. You'll also know that I have an unmet desire in my own head to make real change in the world and that I constantly float between just doing me and not bothering anyone else, and feeling like I am not contributing anywhere near enough.

Maybe writing this means I've tilted to the side that needs to make change in the world. But why me? Who am I to think I have the right to do such a thing? Why do I believe people will listen to me? Why do I want to put myself out there to have my whole character completely pulled apart and ridiculed by those who can't just read something and say, "I don't agree with it," without seeking revenge for its very existence. Feel free to call me 'up myself' but I believe I really am one of the few who can.

I sat with this feeling for a long time. A really long time. Those years of growing up in the eighties, being seen and not heard, being a good child but never better than someone else because that's showing off – how dare I believe I can actually make a difference! Why would I wish to do something more than what everyone else is doing? I don't want to be your saviour, I can only be mine.

The harsh reality remains – there is no-one else that can write this book in this exact way. FACT.

I have an uncanny mix of skills and experiences acquired over this fascinating life. I have a degree in communications. I have extensive experience in media. I have an internal understanding of the complex marriage between public opinion, government and media; how each shapes the other in an often-vicious cycle of one-sided storytelling built on sensationalism. I have further qualifications in the areas of both physical healthcare and spiritual consciousness. I've lived in both Western and Eastern communities.

I personally understand failed health systems as well as how alternative care methods, basic nutrition and exercise can provide real change in lives. I have made extremely hard decisions in my life for the betterment of my physical and mental health. I have been forced to be my own advocate many times. I have a rare medical condition, which may be exacerbated by vaccination and I understand what it's like to be on the other side of justice for doing the right thing. I have been excluded, like many, from living my life, running my business and making an income. I've been locked alone in my house. I've been forced to make hard financial decisions and ostracised for my choices from friends and extended family.

But most importantly, I've also been the person who would've hated this book the most. The person who would strongly disagree with its premise and the information contained within. The person who would have thrown it down after a single sentence and not wanted to engage in a single minute of discussion about a valid yet opposing view. The person who was once so set in their ways, another opinion would have felt like a threat to who I believed myself to be.

I've lived through how hard it is to continue being that judgemental person and I urge you to let that side of you go. It will be the best thing you'll ever do. If I can do it, so can you. This is my attempt to start you off on that journey. But you have to do the work.

I'm not forcing you to change, I'm asking you to consider it, to expand your mind and decide the person you want to be going forward. Are there some parts of you that need to be put down because they are too heavy to continue to carry?

There is a great saying that 'people can only meet you as deeply as they have first met themselves'. That's why I'm putting this to you – because I've been there. I've done the work. Now it's your turn. It was fucking hard but my greatest achievement to date. It's changed everything I do. It's changed who I want to be. It's changed my relationships with people and myself. It's changed my life.

This is an opportunity to write out all your anger, fear and resentment over the last few years. You can speak now. I will listen. Let's start the hashtag #iwilllisten and let every person get how they genuinely felt off their chest without judgement.

Maybe you were scared of people like me – I will listen.

Maybe you were angry at how much school your child missed and how much it continues to affect them – I will listen.

Maybe you were harmed by the vaccine – I will listen.

Maybe you just need to speak for you. Allow yourself that chance.

With the introduction of AI and the rise of media giants filtering out what they decide is misinformation, now may be the most important time to speak and train your body to listen to that instinct in your gut. What if this is the last real chance you get to learn how to process your feelings and traumas so you can hear what your body is really trying to tell you without reacting to those triggers? Don't hide your feelings. Express them. Be real. Be honest. Soon your gut feelings might be the only real truth that remains in this world.

Here are your last journal pages. If you don't have a goal right now, that's fine. If you just want to vent, that's fine too. Feel free to write and write and write. Feel free to highlight text. Do what you want with this book.

I want it to inspire you to do better than yesterday because that's all that anyone can do. None of us can take back the failings of the past. We can only strive to do better. We can only take comfort in the knowledge we now have to make better decisions for tomorrow.

Decide what you most need today and do it. I will listen. You can do it. You can try something new. You can start to make a change and grow – just as life intended. If the Australian band Eskimo Joe[35] can go from 'Sweater' to 'Foreign Land' in a handful of years, you too can 'try to understand it if you can'.

Your turn

Who are you? Are you who you want to be? If not, tomorrow is a new day – what are you going to do with your new start?

The Four Per Cent

Final words

If any part of this book has really cut to your soul, if it has made you sad, if it has made you angry without being dismissive of my part in it, this is because those feelings exist in you already.

And the reason I can bring them out is because they also exist in me.

The reason it feels deep is because I extracted every single comment and description you've just read from the dark place inside me that needed answers. I believe I've found most.

I don't want to be talked about after this. I don't want your first response to be whether you decide I'm right or wrong. I don't want the traditional discussion of what side you are on after taking in these pages.

I want your first response to be to navigate the parts of this story that made you feel something at your core. That's what the journaling along the way was all about. What did you feel? Which lines or topics made you angry or sad? Where did you feel it?

Try and work out what that is telling you.

If it's anger – where is your anger directed? At me? At government? At yourself?

Looking within is the only way forward. Learn to control your own emotions. Decide what is really worth your time. Don't just have a halfhearted impact, make a difference.

This book was not designed to make you feel bad. It wasn't written to judge you. I'm not telling you that you haven't done enough so far. I don't want to make you relive every situation where you were wrong or could have handled things better – we can't go back to a time that has already existed and act differently. We can only move forward.

Ask yourself how you can contribute to the greater good of the world today. It needs you. We all need you.

Acknowledgments

This book is a collection of my thoughts and experiences only made possible by those around me who shaped the person I became.

My first acknowledgement is to my parents. Like all children I rode the journey of joy and embarrassment, acceptance and disapproval with mine. As I aged, I came to appreciate that I couldn't have wanted a better set of parents. I inherited a nice mix of my father's stubbornness and my mother's compassion. I came to learn it was important to share both my father's comfort in isolation and the joy for simple pleasures coupled with my mother's strong sense of community and unwavering love and support for her friends and family. They have taught me valuable life skills and a strong foundation of knowing who I am. My father is not shy in asking questions about the things he doesn't understand and my mother would be genuinely upset if she knew she offended someone. Both traits were equally important to get this book into the world the way it was written.

To my two sisters and four nieces, each one of us so different in our views and ways of experiencing the world. We all have our different stories. Each of you has shaped my own and, as women in this world, may we never shy of voicing it. There is courage to be found in each one of you. Get out there and show the world who you are because you and your story matter. I love you all equally.

To my brother-in-law who I've known since I was six years old, you are often the glue that holds the family together. You are also the glue that holds your community of Churchill together. You are appreciated by many, far more than you know.

To my dear friend Renee, what a journey it has been. You have been in my life since I was twelve years old and I have been shaped as a human by you. We have been so dangerously honest with each other, we have needed time to process the hurt and anger that only a true best friend could inflict out of genuine love and concern. I wouldn't have become who I am today without that. Your level of friendship has been desperately needed. We've tested a lot of hard conversations on each other and survived them all. No matter where we are at, I could still call you in my darkest moment – as I did and mentioned in this book – and you would always know what to say. Without you, I would have no growth as a human or balance of opinion in this world. You truly are the one who can bring me back to the middle when I start swimming to the extremes. Never change.

To my cousin Maree, who I owe for coming to save my life. That Santa photo you gave me in 2010 when you went back a week later to rejoin the line remains one of my prized possessions. You have continued to be the first person on the other end of the phone when I need you the most. Your unconditional love and support will always be appreciated. You are my family but also my oldest friend.

To my dear friend Saffron, you are quite possibly the most compassionate and emotionally intelligent human I know. There are so many things I could say but put simply, the way you conduct yourself inspires me to be a better person.

To dear Trudi. My last day in Melbourne would not have been possible without all your assistance in getting me on that plane. Thank you for being the one who makes me laugh the hardest, especially when I'm feeling down, and for being a better plant mumma to my babies than I could ever be.

To my dearest Leith, my fellow soldier of war during the onslaught of opinions. Neither of us needed the experience but I'm glad we stood in the minority together. Only you can truly understand the pain of it all. I never had to hide who I was. I never had to overthink my conversations. Just true love, support and complete understanding. I needed you. Thank you for being there.

To the friend who held together my sanity during lockdown, Calypso. Such a wonderful friend to make just as lockdown started especially within my '5 km'. Those daily walks, chai runs, pet cuddles,

Acknowledgments

home-cooked meals, and fish-and-chip takeaways were the only things that gave me any sense of normalcy. I loved your super thoughtful picnics in the park with no stone unturned. You truly made the shittiest of times feel very special.

To all my beautiful clients at 'The Balanced Base' who supported me during my transition to online, my six lockdowns and eventual closure. In the early stages, you were not only my sole financial support, you were my sense of purpose in this world. There are too many of you to individually name but I appreciate your patience and understanding, and those of you who scheduled walks and Zoom calls for continued sanity. I will always appreciate you and am lucky enough to still have some of you in my life. Also a shout-out to my life-long friends and family who signed up online, knowing they wouldn't use it. Your weekly financial support was needed and appreciated more than you know.

To my neurologist Dr Hilary Hunt, this is the result of your medical care, your support and those three little words you asked in September 2022. Thank you.

There are so many people who have shaped who I've become over the years. Some old friends, some new ones. Some family, some I grew up calling Auntie and Uncle. Some who are still in contact, some who are not. Some who are still with us, some who have since passed. Be it known that I appreciate the time we had, or continue to share. You've undoubtedly made me a better person.

To those of you who have received those honest letters, I'm sorry for any pain I caused but thank you for unknowingly holding space for me. You will know who you are. If I had my time again, I'd express my feelings with far more compassion for yours. Thank you for the life lesson. It's been valuable.

To the woman who shaped my biggest letter – this book. Kellie, without you I would have been an angry and teary explosion of bad sentences and misplaced apostrophes. You have truly crafted this into what I had in my head but couldn't bring to life as succinctly as I imagined. Thank you.

To every one of you who has made it this far and told your story along with mine. May it heal your soul. Who do you want to acknowledge?

Where to go for more information

The following websites, books and notes contain extra information on a variety of topics, which may be of interest to some readers.

Covid-19 response statistics

https://lockdownstats.melbourne/

https://www.statista.com/topics/6414/coronavirus-covid-19-in-australia/#topicOverview

https://covidlive.com.au/

https://www.aph.gov.au/Parliamentary_Business/Committees/Senate/Legal_and_Constitutional_Affairs/COVID19RC47

https://twitter.com/sharnellevella (Archived summary of the Victorian Government's rules and regulations over the response.)

Trigeminal Neuralgia

https://www.facepain.org/about-fpa/

https://tnaaustralia.org.au/what-is-trigeminal-neuralgia/

Health and wellbeing

The Body Keeps the Score: Mind, Brain and Body in the Transformation of Trauma, Bessel Van der Kolk, published by Penguin Press, 2015

The Myth of Normal: Trauma, Illness & Healing in a Toxic Culture, Dr Gabor Mate with Daniel Mate, published by Vermilion – Mass Market, 2022

Nonviolent Communication: A Language of Life: Life-Changing Tools for Healthy Relationships, Marshall B. Rosenberg, published by Puddledancer Press, 2015

Other

- The four main Covid-19 vaccines in Australia are known by their brand names of AstraZeneca, Pfizer, Moderna and Novavax by the Australian population.
- 'Murdoch Media' is a term used to refer to all of the media entities owned in both Australia and overseas by Rupert Murdoch.
- One Nation is a political party in Australia.
- The Voice to Parliament, was a proposed federal advisory body to comprise of First Nation's people to have input in decisions made directly affecting them. It was rejected in a national referendum of Australians on the 14th October 2023.
- Black Lives Matter, is a social movement started in the US to highlight racial discrimination and inequality.
- Grace Tame and Brittany Higgins are Australian women who spoke out about sexual assault.
- Deceased US entertainer Michael Jackson's life had been marred by allegations of child sexual assault.
- American Actor Kevin Spacey was acquitted of sexual assault in 2023. In the lead up to his trial he was cancelled by international media.
- VicRoads is a Victorian Government joint venture responsible for licensing and registration in the state of Victoria, Australia.
- A $580 million quarantine facility was built in Melbourne due to the Covid-19 pandemic. It opened after lockdown was lifted and only housed 2168 people during the eight months it was open. Most of these people were unvaccinated international arrivals.
- In 2023 The Victorian Government under Daniel Andrews walked away from hosting the 2026 Melbourne Commonwealth Games. The withdrawal cost $589 million to the Victorian taxpayers.
- The Australian Government will spend $9 billion over the next four years to secure nuclear submarines that will arrive between 2030-2050 as part of the AUKUS agreement.
- During the Melbourne lockdown the Premier of Victoria Dan Andrews held a press conference each day. It was widely understood in Melbourne that if he was wearing a 'North Face' jacket it was good news. If he was wearing a suit jacket it was bad news.

Where to go for more information

Endnotes

1. Australian Government, Department of Health, Australia's Covid-19 Vaccine Roadmap. Data as at 22 March 2022 states:
   - >95 % of Victorian's have had one dose
   - 93.7 % considered fully vaccinated with two doses
   - 95 % of Australian's 16 years and over considered fully vaccinated

   https://web.archive.org/web/20220323083732/https://www.health.gov.au/initiatives-and-programs/covid-19-vaccines/numbers-statistics

2. Former Prime Minister Scott Morrison on 2GB radio – 19 August 2020

   https://www.theguardian.com/australia-news/live/2020/aug/19/coronavirus-australia-latest-updates-nsw-security-guard-hotel-quarantine-victoria-testing-daniel-andrews-health-vaccine-live-news?page=with:block-5f3cda848f0-89b3b72acf91d#block-5f3cda848f089b3b72acf91d

3. Former Prime Minister Scott Morrison on 3AW radio with Neil Mitchell. Article by Christopher Knaus in The Guardian 19 August 2020

   https://www.theguardian.com/australia-news/2020/aug/19/scott-morrisons-talk-of-mandatory-covid-vaccine-is-dangerous-experts-warn

4. World Health Organization – Covid-19 and mandatory vaccination: Ethical considerations, published April 2021, republished May 2022.

   https://www.who.int/publications/i/item/WHO-2019-nCov-Policy-brief-Mandatory-vaccination-2021.1

5. Former Minister for Health and Medical Research Brad Hazzard at Covid-19 Live Press Conference, Sydney, NSW Health, press conference archive, 29 July 2021

   https://www.health.nsw.gov.au/Infectious/covid-19/Pages/press-conferences.aspx

6. Former Prime Minister Scott Morrison, *The Guardian* 23 August 2021

   https://www.theguardian.com/australia-news/video/2021/aug/23/pm-scott-morrison-says-australia-must-learn-to-live-with-covid-this-is-not-sustainable-video

7. Former Victorian Premier Dan Andrews, Covid-19 Live Press Conference, Melbourne, 10 NEWS Melbourne, 31 August 2021

   https://www.facebook.com/10NewsMelb/videos/covid-19-press-conference-31-august-2021/2158361447651342

8   Former Victorian Premier Dan Andrews – Covid-19 Live Press Conference, Melbourne, Channel Nine News - 5th September 2021 (Article containing Ch 9 video)

   https://www.express.co.uk/news/world/1486843/Australia-coronavirus-news-Daniel-Andrews-unvaccinated-anti-vax-healthcare-lockdown-vn

   "The Victorian Premier says the state is heading for a 'vaccine economy', here's what that might look like" Judd Boaz, ABC news, 6th September 2021.

   https://www.abc.net.au/news/2021-09-06/daniel-andrews-vaccine-passport-double-vaccinated/100435606

9   Former Prime Minister Scott Morrison, Sky News, 19 Nov 2021

   https://www.news.com.au/finance/work/leaders/i-do-not-need-to-be-lectured-by-scott-morrison-dan-andrews-savages-pm-over-covid-commentary/news-story/1d0b33a85fd3d9310bf37c348bae6644

10 Former Premier Dan Andrews, Covid-19 Live Press Conference, Melbourne, Channel Seven News, 27 January 2022

   https://www.facebook.com/7NEWSMelbourne/videos/victoria-covid-19-update-thursday-27-january-2022/657239172090232/

11 "Pfizer did not know whether Covid vaccine stopped transmission before rollout, executive admits" – Frank Chung, news.com.au, 13 October 2022

   https://www.news.com.au/technology/science/human-body/pfizer-did-not-know-whether-covid-vaccine-stopped-transmission-before-rollout-executive-admits/news-story/f307f28f794e173ac017a62784fec414

   Article contains video of J.Small Pfizer, European Union Parliament, 11 October 2022.

12 'I am absolutely pro-vaccine': Dan Andrews clashes with anti-vaxxer at Midsumma Pride March, Rebecca Borg, news.com.au, 6 Feb 2023

   https://www.news.com.au/national/victoria/politics/i-am-absolutely-provaccine-dan-andrews-clashes-with-antivaxxer-at-midsumma-pride-march/news-story/fc26f2541631376a872fc88dc6f471aa

13 "Unvaxxed mum forced overseas for life saving transplant" – Avi Yemini, Rebel News, 20 July 2023

   https://www.rebelnews.com/unvaxxed_mum_fights_back_after_heartless_hospitals_deny_transplant

14 "Banned covid posts 'totally factual" – Chris Kenny, *The Weekend Australian*, 22 July 2023

   https://www.theaustralian.com.au/subscribe/news/1/?sourceCode=TAWEB_WRE170_a_LIN&dest=https%3A%2F%2Fwww.theaustralian.com.au%2Fnation%2Fmany-censored-social-media-posts-did-not-contain-covid19-misinformation%2Fnews-story%2Fc47a8217ffada2cf576475aef3c12c63&memtype=anonymous&mode=premium&v21=HIGH-Segment-1-SCORE&V21spcbehaviour=append

15 "Family claim Sydney's St Vincent hospital is refusing to give their young daughter a life-saving lung transplant because she won't get Covid jabs" – David Southwell, *Daily Mail Australia*, 1 August 2023

   https://www.dailymail.co.uk/news/article-12359151/Family-claim-Sydneys-St-Vincents-hospital-refusing-young-daughter-life-saving-lung-transplant-wont-Covid-jabs.html

16 "Melbourne public housing tower residents offered $5m payout over covid lockdown", Australian Associated Press, *The Guardian* – 9 May 2023

   https://www.theguardian.com/australia-news/2023/may/09/melbourne-public-housing-tower-residents-win-5m-payout-over-covid-lockdown

17 Thailand U-turns on COVID vaccination rule for visitors" Reuters, 9 January 2023.

   https://www.reuters.com/world/asia-pacific/thailand-rescinds-entry-requirement-proof-covid-vaccination-minister-2023-01-09/

18 Jo Lauder, The Shakeup, Triple J Hack, 15 Sep 2023

   https://www.abc.net.au/triplej/programs/hack/hack/102836594

19 HARI, J. (2019). Chasing the scream: *The first and last days of the War on Drugs*. BLOOMSBURY Publishing.

20 Former QLD Chief Health Officer Dr Jeanette Young, Covid-19 Live Press Conference, Brisbane, ABC Brisbane, 7 October 2021

   https://www.facebook.com/abcinbrisbane/videos/queensland-covid-19-update-october-7-2021/3008448662739891/

21 "Northcote street party erupts after Richmond 'takeaway' pub crawl slammed" *Sunday Herald Sun*, 16 August 2021.

   https://www.heraldsun.com.au/news/victoria/huge-crowds-gather-for-takeaway-pub-crawl/news-story/ed648fff47f72468a0eceeac55c9bbcb

22 Interview Denise Drysdale, *Women's Day*, 15 August 2022.

https://centralneurosurgery.com.au/aussie-tv-treasure-denise-drysdale-opens-up-about-her-secret-brain-surgery-for-trigeminal-neuralgia/

23 2023 National Tour, Australian Medical Professionals' Society, with UK Cardiologist Dr. Aseem Malhotra.

https://amps.redunion.com.au/malhotra_tour2023

24 Interview with Dr. Nick Coatsworth, Today Show, 9 News Australia, 28 February 2024.

https://www.facebook.com/9NewsGoldCoast/videos/court-rules-vaccine-mandate-unlawful/378570841466795/

25 Interview with Dr. Kerryn Phelps, Today Show, 9 News Australia, 21 December 2022.

https://www.youtube.com/watch?v=gRiDgasJDNs

"Dr Kerryn Phelps reveals 'devastating' Covid vaccine injury, says doctors have been censored" Frank Chung, news.com.au, 20 December 2022.

https://www.news.com.au/technology/science/human-body/dr-kerryn-phelps-reveals-devastating-covid-vaccine-injury-says-doctors-have-been-censored/news-story/0c1fa02818c99a5ff65f5bf852a382cf

26 Former Minister for Health and Medical Research Brad Hazzard at Covid-19 Live Press Conference, Sydney, NSW Health, press conference archive – 29 July 2021

https://www.health.nsw.gov.au/Infectious/covid-19/Pages/press-conferences.aspx

27 Dreamer, M.O. (2006) *The invitation*. San Francisco: HarperSanFranciso.

http://www.oriahmountaindreamer.com/

28 Jay Shetty with Dr Gabor Mate – Podcast

https://www.jayshetty.me/podcast/gabor-mate-why-your-trauma-is-showing-up-as-guilt-fear-and-shame-how-to-untrap-yourself-from-the-past

29 Rosenberg, M. B. (2015). *Nonviolent communication: A language of life*. PuddleDancer Press.

30 "Google's search tweaks will help prioritize quality websites in results" Jessica Bursztynsky, Fast Company, 18 August 2022.

https://www.fastcompany.com/90779296/googles-search-tweaks-will-help-prioritize-quality-websites-in-results

31 "Why countries are halting the AstraZeneca shot", Maria Cheng, AP News – 16 March 2021.

https://apnews.com/article/why-countries-stopping-astrazeneca-vaccine-shot-explained-82f4c89a76c21f287e3041b52b7a69f0

32 "Novak Djokovic: Timeline of tennis star's visa saga in Australia." Tom Kershaw, Independent , UK, 17 January 2022.

https://www.independent.co.uk/sport/tennis/novak-djokovic-visa-timeline-australia-b1989306.html

33 Australian Government – TGA - Database of Adverse Event Notifications (DAEN) – medicines

https://daen.tga.gov.au/medicines-search/

34 Australian Bureau of Statistics – Covid-19 Mortality in Australia: Deaths registered until 31 January 2024

https://www.abs.gov.au/articles/covid-19-mortality-australia-deaths-registered-until-31-january-2024

35 Eskimo Joe: 'Sweater' released 1998 by label Troy Horse; 'Foreign Land' released 2009 by label Warner

About the author

Lauren Smith is a mindfulness coach, and a Pilates and yoga instructor who first made a career in Melbourne's television industry. She left the fast-paced lifestyle behind when diagnosed with an incurable cranial nerve disorder. Since then, Lauren has survived brain surgery, rehabbed herself from a spinal injury, and lived through Melbourne's Covid lockdown. Her experiences have led her to advocate for balancing physical and mental wellbeing by learning to tune into your own body.

Lauren now teaches others to rest and recover as much as they push the edges of their comfort zone, and to choose language that helps them communicate and process their feelings effectively with themselves and others. These days, you will find Lauren on the beaches and in the Muay Thai studios of Thailand; or travelling to the next exotic destination, eager to meet the locals and expats and listen to their stories.

www.ingramcontent.com/pod-product-compliance
Lightning Source LLC
Chambersburg PA
CBHW032336300426
44109CB00041B/1069